Unbound By Place or Time:
Museums and Online Learning

Crow, William B., 1973-
  Unbound by place or time : museums and online learning / by William B. Crow and Herminia Din.
    p. cm.
  Includes index.
  ISBN 978-1-933253-12-1 (alk. paper)
  1. Museums--Educational aspects. 2. Web-based instruction. 3. Museums--Information technology. 4. Museum techniques. 5. Museums--Educational aspects--Case studies. 6. Web-based instruction--Case studies. 7. Museums--Information technology--Case studies. 8. Museum techniques--Case studies. I. Din, Herminia, 1968- II. Title.
  AM7.C77 2009
  069'.15--dc22
                        2009011016

Unbound By Place or Time: Museums and Online Learning

By WILLIAM B. CROW and HERMINIA DIN

The AAM PRESS

AMERICAN ASSOCIATION OF MUSEUMS

1575 EYE STREET NW. SUITE 400
WASHINGTON DC 20005

WWW.AAM-US.ORG

Contents

Acknowledgments

|

We began our collaboration in museum-based online teaching in 2006. While we both previously had experience as online educators in a higher education context (at that time, online learning had already been embraced by universities for well over a decade), we noticed a lack of qualitative, learner-centric online teaching and learning offered by museums. We decided to experiment with this methodology in a museum context, and created an interactive online workshop for elementary-level teachers, "Face to Face: Comparing Portraits," offered by the Metropolitan Museum of Art in the summer of 2007. This blended online and onsite workshop included asynchronous interaction (threaded discussion, collaborative wiki projects, blogging), synchronous, real-time webinars and an in-person workshop with the original works of art. Two years later, we continue to create and teach online workshops for teachers, as well as online programs directly with students, either as a means to complement their in-person visit to the museum or as stand-alone educational experiences. At this writing, we have reached hundreds of students and teachers from 28 states, six countries, and four continents.

The uniqueness of this collaboration is a true distance learning experience —in Anchorage and New York City. We communicate via different online tools—email, Skype, Elluminate, Epsilen, Voicethread, GoogleDocs, Flickr—but more important than the tools, we have discovered new ways of collaborating and connecting with one another and with others. With the support of the Metropolitan Museum of Art and its funders, we are grateful to have this opportunity to explore what online learning and teaching can bring to the field of museum education. Humbly, we would like to share our experiences in online learning, which has culminated in the publication of this book, in the spirit of starting a dialogue in the museum community about the powerful educational possibilities that online learning can offer.

We could not have accomplished this without the collaboration, expertise and passion of our colleagues, to whom we extend our sincere gratitude. We would like to express our appreciation to the contributors to each of the case studies, without whom we could not have completed this publication. We also thank the Educational Enterprise Zone (EEZ) at New York Institute of Technology for their generous tech support and hosting of all our Elluminate webinar sessions. We also would like to thank John Strand and Susan Levine of The AAM Press at the American Association of Museums for thoroughly understanding the need for this book, their editorial and design expertise and their words of publishing wisdom throughout the process. We also express our deepest appreciation to Selma Thomas for her gracious support and advice.

Finally, we would like to thank our families, in particular Philip Kain and Darrell Bailey, for their support and encouragement.

WILLIAM B. CROW and HERMINIA DIN

Foreword

BY MARY ELLEN MUNLEY

This book gave me a glimpse of the future of museum education and it is good. In fact, it is better than good. The future of museum education is terrifically exciting. William B. Crow's and Herminia Din's book is a tour de force. *Unbound By Place or Time: Online Learning and Museums* is a welcome contribution to the field from two impressive young professionals and a must-read for anyone working with museums and interested in maximizing their public value.

Those worried that museums will become obsolete in our increasingly technological world will be comforted by Crow's and Din's sophisticated analysis of the complex interplay between on-site and online experiences. "In the end, tools are tools," they argue. They challenge the reader to view both the built environment of a museum and the online environment of a museum as equally important (yet different) learning tools. The value of the museum does not lie in the tools per se; the value lies in the capacity of the museum to provide equitable access to meaningful learning for all interested people. That value is only increased by the introduction of the new online tools.

The brilliance of this book comes in its underlying reliance on the foundations of progressive education and best practices in museum education. Online learning environments provide a powerful set of new tools for museum educators guided by a learner-centric and participatory approach to teaching and learning. The foundations of museum education work from its earliest days—equitable access and assisting people to make personal connections—remain the foundations of museum education in the world of new technologies.

It is evident that the authors are master teachers. Though they clearly have knowledge of all the wiz-bang tools of the online world, they provide a primer for beginners. You will find concise definitions of everything from wikis and Ning groups to threaded discussions and digital drop boxes. There is also a useful chapter on how to get started. Better still, the authors provide examples of the use of blogs, online course management and more by museums.

But being prepared for (and leading) the future of museum education is more than familiarity with these new tools. Just as in past generations, there is a revolution afoot within the ranks of museum education, and Crow and Din are in the forefront of this one. The introduction of online technologies, they instruct us, forces attention to some basic questions: Where is the museum? Where and who is your audience? When is the museum "open" and available? In short, these new technologies will redefine the role of the museum in society.

Our future—thanks to pervasive online technologies—will be one of greater access and deeper understanding of our visitors; deeper, longer and more frequent interactions between visitors and staff; multiple voices, multiple perspectives and respect for various types of expertise. And the future of museum education will still be grounded in collections and the power of learning from artifacts using interactive, learner-centric methods. It sounds terrific—but it will not happen overnight, and it will not happen without struggle.

Crow and Din pepper their explication of opportunity with much appreciated reality checks. Sharing blogs with the public requires addressing standards for writing and procedures for editing; teacher-produced learning activities question practices about review and approval of museum-associated work; participating in learning communities with expectations for longevity, respect, trust and customization requires examining staff roles and responsibilities. None of it will be easy. But the future envisioned by Crow and Din makes it all but irresistible to give it our best try.

Mary Ellen Munley is principal, MEM Associates.
She was formerly the Director of Education at The Field Museum, Chicago.

Introduction

W e live and work in a world of ever-changing digital technologies. While there is still a substantial global digital divide, it is clear that we are increasingly interconnected, relying on digital means of communication and collaboration. We seek out information online, we plan both our work-related matters and leisure time activities by consulting the Internet and increasingly we use the online environment to connect with our friends, families and communities. Travel arrangements are made to faraway places, vacation photos are uploaded and shared, personal blog entries are created and commented upon and social networks are developed and expanded. We are truly immersed in a digital, participatory culture in both our working and personal lives.

Since the early 1990s, the Internet has also become a portal for museum access: a gateway for the dissemination of collection information, exhibit materials and image repositories. Museums continue to build their online presence and now consider websites not only as a means to distribute information to visitors, but as a place where online visitors can learn about the collection, gather images and documents and even join an online social network.

It is easy to understand why museums have embraced online spaces as a means to expand their presence. Usability, cost efficiency, multimedia features, and most importantly, speed and effectiveness in communicating with audiences are all compelling strengths that the Internet offers. These factors can also inspire museums to consider how their online presence can be not only a marketing tool, but also how it can inform, expand or complement the in-person museum visit. Often led by museum educators, online resources for visitors have expanded and diversified. Publications, online features for children and families, video and even links to shared content on websites such as Flickr and YouTube are ubiquitous in many museums. Podcasts and blogs have started to grow in museums, allowing for new channels of two-way communication between the museum and its visitors.

As the presence of technology has increased and technology's interactive nature grown, we have seen a rise in the learner-centric model of museum education practice. By learner-centric, we mean attention is focused on the learner's needs, abilities, interests and learning styles, with the teacher as a facilitator of learning. Historically museums considered that the mere act of opening their doors to the public constituted a sound educational effort. Now museums must take a much more active role in engaging and involving their visitors and communities. Using learner-centric approaches, museums can value the diverse backgrounds and experiences of their visitors. They can see the educational experience not as a mandate to act as cognoscenti handing down information to passive, grateful visitors, but as an open-ended interaction that connects in meaningful ways with the visitors' own ideas, opinions and interpretations.

We see a rise in learner-centric models of museum education and the increasingly participatory nature of online technologies as very compatible trends. In addition to the positive aspects of access, economy and visibility, the Internet offers a multitude of tools that can enrich and deepen a learner's encounter with the museum. Educational experiences in these online environments can bring together peoples from diverse geographic areas and backgrounds and allow them the necessary time to have thoughtful, considered conversations with both museum professionals and their peers. The range of communication tools offered in online environments—chat, text, multimedia, live conversation—expands the possibilities of connecting learners to environments that they find most useful and comfortable.

Alternative delivery methods of museum education are not a new phenomenon. For decades museum educators have traveled beyond the walls of the museum to teach in schools, community centers, libraries and senior living facilities, using slides and reproductions as a way to introduce museum collections to offsite audiences. Videoconferencing and teleconferencing have served as bridges, allowing visitors to experience the museum across cities and even countries. Traditional videoconferencing began as a means of broadcasting content to an audience of learners. Now, however, it is adapting to new tools and new pedagogies that are more interactive in nature and responsive to new learners who have come to expect more involvement in the learning process. We also now see hybrid programs that combine videoconferencing with Web-based interaction that allows participants to interact with museum staff face-to-face and access the site-based online resources at other times.

Given these recent phenomena—the rise of the learner-centric model of museum education and the increasingly participatory nature of the Internet—some important questions arise for museums. How might museums harness the interactive qualities of the online environment as tools for active teaching and learning for diverse learners and communities, rather than creating websites that essentially broadcast the same information to many? Can museums turn their attention to smaller communities of learners, narrowcasting to these constituencies, in order to involve them and—very importantly—learn from them? How can museums engage visitors in deep, qualitative experiences that encourage them to visit the museum in person and/or further explore online resources?

As the Internet expands and delivery methods grow, museums can add these questions to the growing list: Because online learning unfolds over minutes, days, weeks or months, how does that ongoing nature affect visitor participation, the perception of the collections and the format of education programs? What is the role of the museum in these online education encounters? How can museums balance their own expertise and resources with greater visitor participation and "user-generated content?" What possibilities exist for a blurring of online and on-site programming and what advantages does this blended approach offer for museum education?

This book will examine these questions, as well as a variety of current practices and future possibilities for interactive online learning that can be adapted for a range of museums. How museums address the interactive tools of the Internet will have a profound effect on museum education. One of our intended audiences is museum educators, of course. But we also intend this book to be useful to every museum professional involved in education and public programs, broadly speaking. We draw first upon our experience working with K-12 teachers and students, as these visitors have been our primary focus in our work. But ultimately we want to engage a broader clientele in the museum experience. We have included examples and suggestions of how online learning can reach broader audiences.

This book does not devote attention to hardware, software, specific websites or digital tools. References to these are kept to a minimum. While these might be useful and are necessary components of creating online learning experiences, they evolve on an almost daily basis. Instead we have chosen to focus on the interactive principles of online learning and the pedagogies that we have found to be useful. Museum educators already possess the skills and knowledge to engage visitors in a wide range of interactive educational experiences. This book is an invitation to all museum professionals to explore in their own institutions the rich possibilities of online education.

CHAPTER 1

A Multiplicity of Museum Experiences

Museums invite visitors to explore collections through a variety of interactions. Visitors may join group experiences such as public talks or tours, scholarly lectures and symposia, or drop-in weekend family programs. They may read wall labels and didactic panels, listen to audio tours, sketch and take notes, explore hands-on displays and interactive kiosks. During their visit they may enjoy the company of family, friends and museum staff or they may choose to spend their time alone in the galleries. Some visitors spend just a few minutes in a museum, moving quickly through the galleries and visiting a few objects. Other visitors might spend an entire day in one area of the collection. Museums value the diverse experiences that occur in their institutions, and are eager to facilitate experiences that are tailored to their visitors' needs and interests.

When we go online to access the Internet, we have an experience similar to a museum visit. On the Web we engage in an active process of seeking, selecting, scanning and immersing ourselves in a variety of experiences. We browse, search, select and discover. We go online to connect with friends, families and communities, or we can spend time alone. We sometimes get frustrated when we are not able to locate what we are seeking. And sometimes we delight in an unexpected find.

Of course there are clear differences between browsing Web pages and wandering through the halls of a museum. Although digital technologies have increased in their sophistication and aesthetics, they cannot replace the experience of standing in front of an original Velázquez oil painting, the moment of reading original documents penned by our nation's founders or gazing up at a massive, fossilized dinosaur skeleton. While there is no substitute for these experiences, the Internet can be a very real extension of the museum experience and a place that similarly values communication and visitor engagement. It invites feedback and offers a wide spectrum of ways for the visitor to connect and contribute. Like museums, the Internet is in the process of constant change, reevaluation and renewal as websites are added, reviewed, edited and reorganized. Information and research changes just as visitors change.

As our daily lives become more rooted in digital communications and interactions, it is becoming clear that museums and visitors can find new ways of intersecting and interacting in an online format. The interactive qualities of the Web, which allow and even demand user input, can facilitate meaningful, personal and educational experiences with the collections. In this chapter we define what online learning currently means and what it might mean in the future to educational experiences in museums.

WHAT IS ONLINE LEARNING?

Educators, scientists and scholars have been developing and researching methodologies for teaching via alternative delivery systems often discussed under the umbrella term *distance learning*. Building on the effectiveness of educational broadcasting in radio and television, educators began to utilize telecommunication networks to connect with learners. Videoconferencing, a technology developed in the 1980s and still used today by a number of museums, allowed museum educators to be seen and heard on a type of closed-circuit television, while students in the school setting could be seen and heard by the educators.

Digital learning, or the exchange of information using computer technology in networked environments, has a history that dates prior to widespread use of the Internet, when users across distant geographic areas were first beginning to communicate using simple electronic bulletin boards and early forms of chat through connected systems. These pioneering efforts, often created and led by university researchers, scientists and scholars, were a means to offer a computer-based campus for faculty and researchers in higher education. By the 1990s, when the Internet began to blossom and increasingly visual user interfaces made the online world more user-friendly, the development of online course management systems (CMS) allowed universities to offer alternate formats of course delivery, primarily as a means of distance education for students living away from the physical campus. Although these developments began to connect faculty and students in new ways, online learning, also at times called e-learning, was sometimes seen as a second-rate version of an in-person classroom experience—less rigorous and a poor substitute for the on-campus course.

Online learning is no longer seen as a substitute for the in-person encounter or a less desirable alternative, but rather a new way for educators and learners to interact across time and space. Many universities have embraced online learning and greatly expanded their course offerings. Online learning in higher education now takes many forms, including:

- **Technology-enhanced Courses:** Classes meet primarily face-to-face, but with online components that allow for continuous interaction. For example, an instructor might post a syllabus and a few documents online for the participants to access, but the interaction occurs primarily in person.

- **Hybrid, or Blended Courses:** Combines both online interaction with some face-to-face interaction. For example, a group might use online threaded discussion, blogs and wikis over a 15-week period, but also will meet five times in person during the course of the program.

- **Fully Online Courses:** Educational experiences that occur entirely online, and participants may never meet face-to-face.

Beyond the university environment, other types of institutions have started to experiment with online interaction through group collaboration, online training and conferences that take place at one's desk through live webcasts and webinars. Business, industry and government have followed, developing online solutions for updating and enhancing the skills of workers, mid-level management and executives.

As online learning has expanded and become more accepted, pedagogies and best practices have developed for instructors teaching in this new and ever-expanding environment. Workshops and publications are now offered specifically about the various strategies for engaging students online and recommendations have been made about how to avoid the various pitfalls that online teaching can bring. While the approaches to teaching online can vary widely, a central idea remains at the heart of these new pedagogical practices: online learning is not about translating an in-person experience.

As museum professionals, we understand that it is not possible or desirable to directly translate the in-person museum experience into another format, including online. There are qualities that original objects have—the luminescence of a beautifully painted landscape or the wonderfully dark and musty aroma of a historic house from the 18th century. These have to be experienced in person. Further, the act of experiencing these objects within the walls of buildings that have their own appeal and histories is unique and irreproducible. As the visitor enters a bright sun-filled gallery of paintings, or a dim and mysterious series of vitrines containing a study collection, the sensory and experiential qualities of the encounter should not be simulated or under-valued.

Similar to the physical spaces of galleries or museum, online environments have their own appeal and value. The mutable, flexible qualities of a website can be manipulated to create spaces that are designed with the visitor in mind. Possibilities for placing digital images, resources and communications are nearly infinite in scope. Multimedia such as audio, video and interactive games can offer experiences that are often impractical to achieve within the physical spaces of the museum. In the following section, we will examine a number of reasons why online learning offers a rich landscape for learning in museums, either as a complement to existing on-site programming or as unique, stand-alone educational experiences.

WHY ONLINE LEARNING FOR MUSEUMS?

As museum professionals we focus much of our attention on the encounters that visitors have within the walls of our buildings, but we know that the museum experience begins long before the visitor enters the museum building. Visitors learn about museums from other people, from billboards and brochures, radio and television and of course the Internet. They begin to formulate ideas and responses to their experience before the encounter with the exhibition or collections. They reflect on their childhood experiences in museums if they have visited these institutions before. Additionally, we know that visitors carry their experiences with them long after the actual visit to the museum, often making connections or seeing relationships months or even years after their encounter with the physical collections.[1]

For the past 25 years, museums have been grappling with various means of offering different learning experiences for visitors, many times to reach visitors who physically cannot enter the museum. Some of these programs have utilized very low-tech solutions. Beginning in the 1980s at the Metropolitan Museum of Art, volunteer educators sent booklets of color reproductions of works of art to senior citizens who were unable to visit the museum. Then the educator had a one-on-one telephone conversation with the visitor about the works of art. Later in the early '90s, videoconferencing began to be used by a number of museums. Often led by just one or two staff members, videoconferencing programs connected museums with visitors, primarily students, across distant geographic areas, and in many cases, with steadily increasing participants. *Sea Trek*, a program offered by the Mote Marine Laboratory in Sarasota, Florida, and administered by only one museum educator and one technical administrator, has seen a rise in program participants from 10,000 students in 2006 to over 20,000 in 2008-09. It serves schools across the United States and Canada.

However, the challenges of traditional videoconferencing have become apparent. Similar to other types of broadcast communication, connections between provider and audience must be tested in advance and are often plagued by poor connections or dropped signals. Image and sound quality, while acceptable, is often grainy or pixilated. In addition, because video-conferencing requires setting up a type of mini-television studio within the museum for broadcast, space becomes an issue. Videoconferencing providers have sometimes utilized spaces not much larger than a storage closet, but often find themselves creating backdrops, rolling carts of objects or scenery, in order to heighten the effect for the audience. Another challenge for videoconferencing is the specialized equipment (a codec) required for both the provider and the participant, limiting the number of schools or other audiences that can access these distance-learning programs. But the biggest challenge is the associated expense of equipment and trained technical staff.

Some museums have used a combined approach—integrated video-conferencing with a traditional on-site visit (either as a pre-visit or post-visit experience), while others are combining videoconferencing with online interaction. Colonial Williamsburg has combined the use of videoconferencing with online discussion boards so that participants may begin an interactive dialogue with museum staff before and after their live session with a historic 18th-century character using first-person interpretative approaches. At the heart of these developments in distance learning is the ever-increasing need for learning experiences to involve the participants more deeply.[2] Online learning environments, coupled with experienced and knowledgeable educators, offer this possibility.

The Shift from Broadcasting to Interaction
In the 1990s, museums and other organizations, businesses and even individuals began to establish an online presence as part of standard operating procedure. These initial Web pages met the basic needs of communication, and included important visitor information. Later, museums began to display their collections online and added text from wall labels as

well as materials for educators. Museums initially treated the Internet as a type of additional display case—an efficient and cost-effective gathering place for all types of information. Today, rather than seeing the Web as a rotating billboard or transmitting a one-directional signal to visitors who decide to either accept or reject our message, museums can use the Internet as a vehicle for learning and also as a means to learn more about our visitors and ourselves. Museums must begin to see their online presence as a way to involve and interact with visitors.

The question of broadcasting versus interaction in museums is not restricted to online environments. Museums and museum educators have been exploring the role of interactive, inquiry-based conversation with visitors for the better part of the last century. They see their museum collections not only as objects to be studied but also as assets for visitors to experience and enjoy.[3] It is no longer viable for museums simply to place their collections on view and invite interested visitors to partake. Many museums no longer accept that lecturing to large, passive audiences is an effective means to educate or engage visitors. As we see in the writings of the philosopher John Dewey, as well as visionary researchers such as Lev Vygotsky and Jean Piaget, we must acknowledge and connect with the unique experiences and backgrounds of the individuals in our museums in order to facilitate meaningful and lasting educative experiences.[4]

An essential component of this learner-centric, or constructivist, teaching approach is the tenet that education cannot be "one size fits all." As Howard Gardner explains in his much-heralded theory of multiple intelligences, there is a range of learning styles and educators must be cognizant of the differentiated and diverse learners that we encounter.[5] Effective and meaningful educational experiences cannot rely on the methodology of broadcasting to the mass public, since there is no mass public. Rather, there is a spectrum of distinct individuals, as well as learning communities, that are tied together in very different ways. These communities may self-define by profession, cultural background, location and geography or interest.[6] Acknowledging these distinct communities is not a means of dividing or separating our visitors. On the contrary, it is a new way to encourage visitors with similar ideas and interests to come together and interact with our institutions.

Because online learners may access a learning experience wherever they can access a computer and the Internet, and because individuals may join online communities in any number of ways and on any number of topics, there is vast potential for museums to consider these visitor niches in new ways. Moving beyond efforts to broadcast their presence to a wide and diverse public, museums should also consider how they might connect to smaller communities of learners to involve them in educational

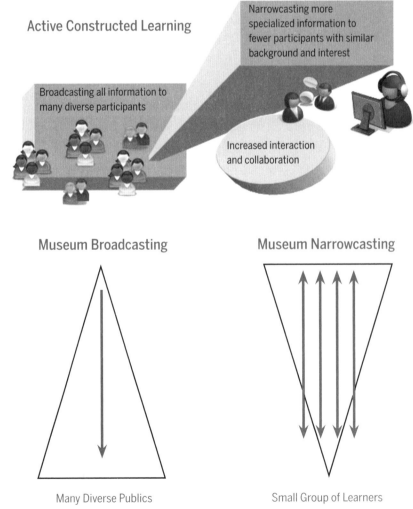

Fig 1: Interaction and Collaboration Increase in Narrowcasting

experiences. This targeting of a specific community, termed *narrowcasting* by the fields of marketing and advertising in the 1980s, is again coming to the fore in the realm of new media.

Narrowcasting, often referring to a business model to market to niche audiences or audience segments, can be embraced by museums to locate and interact with visitors. Sometimes referred to as "the right message at the right time to the right audience," parallels can be seen to several core tenets in the education field. Preparedness to learn, free-choice learning and developmentally "appropriate" methodologies in teaching are all components of education that have much in common with the notion of narrowcasting.

Increased access to the Internet, more content available to users and expanded interaction has effectively moved us from the Information Age to the Collaboration Age. We are no longer passive recipients of information. Instead we can seek out others of like mind and interest, share information and perhaps collaborate on projects over time and space. We want to shape the information that we receive, choose when we want to receive it and be able to respond to it. Today our challenge is less about a search for facts and more about a way to find meaning, to network and to connect to a community. As Thomas Friedman describes in *The World is Flat*, the future is not about production or about being a clearinghouse of information. We are entering an age that allows for unprecedented participation and collaboration.[7]

In narrowcasting, participation and collaboration increase among smaller groups of people with like interests. See Fig 1.

The possibilities for online interaction and exchange with our publics clearly have brought new challenges to the museum field. Museums are grappling with this new and ever-increasing pluralism of voices, ideas and interpretations. Traditionally, museums have been seen as pillars of trust and knowledge, experts at imparting their insider's knowledge to the public at large. Today they are attempting to embrace this new level of widespread participation while maintaining an appropriately authoritative voice.

Balancing greater public participation with the museum's authoritative voice and its hard-earned public trust is not simple. Some museums have stalled in their efforts to use online interaction as a means to connect with their visitors. Many others, however, are advancing. These museums recognize the importance of engagement as a long-term strategy and realize that online learning can provide a rewarding and expansive landscape for learning.

A. Access and Outreach

Two primary reasons for embracing online learning in the museum are access and outreach. Visitors who can access a museum's website can get a sense of the institution, its collections, its scope and even its services before, during and after their visit. Numerous visitors find their way into our collections online through both direct and indirect means. As our collections are tagged and labeled online and become more easily searchable, we find visitors—both online and in-person—who are more familiar with our collections.

For some museums with a national or international mission, access and outreach expand the possibilities of interaction to a much larger scale. Because visitors from around the world may access the museum's website, institutions have the capability of connecting with a vast, new international audience. In addition, institutions with a local or regional focus may find that their museum's new online presence places them in contact with new visitors who may not have been familiar with the museum. The Internet offers great opportunities to develop relationships with potential visitors, members and advocates from the region.

The Internet is used by a wide array of people, not only those who are often cited as digital natives. Seniors use the Internet and email as a vital connection to their families, friends and the world. Teachers and students of all grades use the Internet to search for information, prepare lessons or homework. People who have limited mobility or cannot travel extensively have found the Web to be a place of community, interaction and engagement. In short, the Web has the power to bring visitors virtually to museums, and to have these visitors form a community of learners around the institution.

B. Online Learning Taps Underutilized Resources

Another important benefit of online learning is the opportunity to make use of existing resources that often are simply not available or are under utilized in traditional on-site programming. Consider the digital images of your institution's collections—detail images, *in situ* photography, X-rays from conservation or historical portraits of the founding members. Maps, charts, diagrams and timelines, when used effectively, can illuminate a complex topic for a visitor in ways that dialogue cannot. These supportive materials bring increased value to the museum encounter. Many times they can be easily incorporated into online museum encounters.

Museums have something more to offer in an online environment: their professional staff. While universities and other learning institutions may tap into a museum's collections for the teaching of various subjects, consider the potential of the museum's own professional staff as a body of teachers. Museum educators might partner with conservators who can share their expertise about the art and science of materials. Or they might join with curators who specialize in particular topics, or with museum librarians or archivists who bring new resources to light.

Collaborations between museum educators and other staff members occur frequently in museums today. Museums offer gallery talks given by staff, panel discussions and workshops for teachers. The unique qualities of the Web and digital environments permit and even encourage new types of collaboration between internal museum staff and with external colleagues. Consider a guest speaker from abroad who would have been the perfect addition to an educational program but was not able to travel because of time or money. Online collaborators share information, collectively edit lessons and activities and communicate with visitors individually or as a group. As these collaborations in learning occur over time and space and involve current and potential visitors, they are helping to dissolve many of the traditional barriers to quality educational experiences.

C. Economy, Flexibility and Ease of Use

As museum professionals, we are fully aware of the expense and limited availability of our physical galleries and classroom spaces. Online environments are offered at little or no cost and can be installed locally or hosted by an online service provider. The open source movement, along with freeware and shareware on the Internet, offer an incredibly diverse array of learning environments and tools. In addition, a number of proprietary online learning environments and systems can be licensed with fees. While the ongoing debate about the true value of open source versus proprietary platforms is beyond the scope of this book, museums should consider the cost-benefit relationship of both, bearing in mind that even free tools require the time and expertise of staff to manage.[8]

Another asset that online environments offer is flexibility, as users can make changes to data and design instantaneously. We can avoid the thousand printed copies that are immediately outdated. Besides being a much greener solution to our multitude of printed brochures, teacher resource packets, articles and other analog resources, the digital environment allows our content to be current and updated as frequently as we choose. As we create online spaces for learning for different types of visitors, we can upload the most current information on a topic and add images taken in the exhibition as it opened. We can even add thoughts and materials to our interaction during or after the learning experience has occurred, so that our visitors can continue to learn and use the museum.

Finally, online environments are increasingly easier to use both for the educator and the learner. In the past, computer programming skills were needed to write complex codes. Today it is no longer a requirement to key in HTML or other computer languages. With "What You See Is

What You Get" (WYSIWYG) editing tools and intuitive visual design, program development has been made easier for everyone.

D. The Ability to Document and Archive: A Mirror for Our Visitors and Ourselves

Perhaps one of the greatest opportunities for online learning belongs to us: a chance to learn more about our museum visitors by capturing and documenting interaction. Rather than relying solely on quantitative data about the gate count or even demographic and psychographic data about those who have already visited, online learning can help us understand our visitors even before they enter the museum. Now we can connect with these visitors and ask them about their interests and ideas as we develop programs. We can test, develop and pilot educational programs with accessible and accurate data. These online interactions can document participants' reactions, thoughts and opinions and help us to know a learner's pre-program knowledge of a topic as we observe how initial notions develop into complex ideas.

E. Online Learning Reflects How Our Visitors Communicate

As the use of e-mail, instant messaging, web conferencing, texting and other digital means of communication increases, museums should be responsive not only to how these new technologies function but also how they are transforming the ways that people interact and communicate. Since museums place great value on communicating with visitors by "speaking their language" both literally and metaphorically, we should examine and learn from these new methods of creating dialogue. Although it is not normally the museum's function to teach technology skills, the new types of social, informal learning experiences that museums can now offer help to create a safe social space for the novice visitor to interact and learn from others.

ALL EXPERIENCES ARE AUTHENTIC

At the beginning of the 20th century, with the rise of mechanical repro- duction such as new printing methods and the mass dissemination of photographs, the German philosopher Walter Benjamin argued that the aura of the unique work of art would be diminished. He argued that this phenomenon was not entirely negative, since the "aura" related to societal and economic class, cultural mythologies and rituals and ties to a specific individual, often acting as barriers between the object and mass audiences. Benjamin, along with others of the Frankfurt School such as Theodor Adorno, were concerned but also appreciative of the new possibilities of objects being reproduced in the mechanical age.[9] These philosophical concerns have escalated to a degree unimagined by these early 20th century thinkers as we now find ourselves immersed in a digital world that extends across all geographic borders and political ideologies.

A central idea in Benjamin's writing, one that is highlighted in today's discussions of digital media, is authenticity. We hear online environments described as "simulated worlds." Because virtual environments on the Internet are constructed, they are sometimes labeled inauthentic. Virtual worlds, it is said, cannot compare to our in-person worlds, our physical interactions or our face-to-face encounters. But perhaps they should not be compared. They are simply different. Museums are charged with caring for, preserving and fostering appreciation for real objects—a Shaker chair, a charcoal drawing, a Model T Ford. The experience of being in front of these objects in the museum building is unique and central to museums. However, we should not neglect the fact that there is a world of experiences integral to the experience of the object—its context and history, biography about the maker or owner, its relationship to the world and to our visitors. All of these facets can be explored online.

In the past, critics of online learning posited these interactions to be impersonal, even anonymous because digital platforms allow individuals to present themselves in different ways or even assume different identities. In the early history of online interaction, it was true that opportunities for creating social presence were limited. Today we find that in meaningful interactive online teaching and learning, participants have opportunities to share their experiences, their backgrounds, their ideas and opinions in ways that sometimes go beyond our traditional in-person encounters. Participants, who typically may not voice their opinions in a group in the museum, may reveal their inner dialogue online in a way that provides rich communication with the group and the instructor.

Visitors want to shape and share the experiences in their lives, including their museum experiences. Rather than being "served" as we often discuss in museum terms, visitors want to participate and even have transformative, memorable experiences.[10] Online interaction and learning allows, even demands, this level of participation and offers a new and expansive environment for museums to explore.

Obstacles as Opportunities |

Here is a case study that captures the challenges and rewards in developing our first online learning experience with teachers at the Metropolitan Museum of Art. While this example is specific to elementary-level teachers, we hope that you will find it useful as you consider the possibilities that online learning can offer museums. The tools, teaching approaches and implications presented in this case study will be addressed in more detail in the subsequent chapters of this book.

Teacher programs at the Metropolitan Museum of Art (MMA) are designed to introduce K-12 educators to works of art through object-based learning, interdisciplinary integration and inquiry. Museum educators encourage teachers to pursue further study and contemplation of works of art, directing teachers to the museum's website for additional research. While the online resources are extensive—images, educator guides, a *Timeline of Art History*, multimedia Web features—they have always been seen as separate from the in-person museum experience or as supplemental information.

In early 2007, the final phase of construction on the new Ruth and Harold D. Uris Center for Education limited the number of on-site education programs, yet expanded the new technological infrastructures that would deepen the possibilities for future online educational pro-grams. This crossroads moment—the simultaneous physical obstacle of construction and digital opportunity of expansion—was the catalyst to investigate and eventually embrace Web 2.0 tools: blogs, wikis, threaded discussions and real-time interaction to create an online workshop for teachers.

This first MMA online teacher workshop would not replace the existing on-site encounters with works of art. Rather, it would harness new technologies in a way that would immerse participants from many different geographic areas in the museum's online resources, introduce them to inquiry-based teaching methods and encourage them to create their own classroom materials, all within the museum paradigm.

An Online Encounter of a Unique Kind

From January to June 2007, William Crow and Herminia Din, both museum educators, collaborated to build the activities and frameworks for conversations that would occur during the workshop. In New York, Crow began to develop the pedagogical approach and online activities, while Din, in Alaska, began formatting and preparing the online environment and tools that would contain these elements. Two online services were employed for both the development of the workshop and its implementation—Epsilen Global Learning System[11] (for the asynchronous interaction) and Elluminate Live[12] (for synchronous webinars). This process of co-creating the learning modules progressed over several months with many collegial conversations. This long-distance collaboration was a learning process in itself.

In early July, after receiving applications from potential teacher participants by promoting the workshop through e-mails blasts and online teacher forums, *Face to Face: Comparing Portraits* was launched. The participants consisted of 28 elementary-level educators from 16 states in the U.S., and one educator in a school in Dubai, U.A.E. They possessed a broad range of technology skills, from the novice user of e-mail and Web browsing to those who had experience developing Web pages or online forums for their schools. During the two-week workshop, participants were engaged in a variety of experiences—synchronous and asynchronous, creative and responsive, personal and collective. Teachers wrote blog entries, contributed to threaded discussion topics, created hands-on art projects, collaborated in wikis to craft comparative questions about the works of art, gathered key pieces of information about portraits from across collection areas, and "met" one another in four live, synchronous webinar sessions. By the conclusion of the online interaction, the teachers had worked together to create several PowerPoint resources of images, inquiry-based questions and comparisons and activities that they had adapted. All these could be used with their students and were created collaboratively with materials, images and resources found on the museum's website.

A third of the participants were able to travel to New York on July 31 to participate in a concluding in-person workshop at the museum so that they could experience the original works of art in person. Because these teachers were familiar with the imagery and subject matter of these works and had been immersed in information, activities and inquiry-based questions, we immediately noticed that their conversations quickly moved to deep investigation of the objects. They noticed materials and textures, issues of size and scale and the object's relationship to other works in the gallery environment. The teachers also were able to draw comparisons between objects that had been explored during the online workshop and made reference to contextual information and classroom resources that they would either incorporate or adapt for their students. Primed for their experience in the museum by having participated in the online workshop beforehand, these teachers were prepared to take the conversation to many places and to many levels.

After the intensive two weeks of online interaction and at the closure of the in-person workshop, we re-read the teachers' blog entries and wikis and watched recordings of the four live webinar sessions. We also spent time reviewing the classroom resources that the teachers had created. We began to see that the online workshop, with Web 2.0 tools as vehicles for our interactions, was not merely a means to create a different type of museum learning experience. It was a way to encourage reflection, collaboration and community building that could inform and even change our own museum education practice.

Blogs and Reflective Practice

A blog is unique in that, unlike a personal journal, it is also open to a group of people and can communicate reactions and experiences more immediately to a larger audience, both in written and multimedia form. As participants created entries over days and weeks, each blog provided a personal reflective space, apart from the synchronous group activity, but still connected to the museum and its collections. This tool enabled the participants to examine their own relationship to the works of art, to the online workshop and to the museum. This intermingling of the personal and the public revealed the participants' inner dialogue, as we can see in this example from an Arkansas teacher who is struggling to reconcile two very different aspects of the Gilbert Stuart painting *Mathilda Stoughton de Jaudenes:*

> The main thing I can't figure out about this painting is the background. The table with the books makes sense, as does the chair the lady is sitting on, but it seems the billowing curtain and blue sky are out of place. Although the blue of the sky repeats the blue of the dress and the gold in the curtain repeats the gold embroidery of the dress —both creating a certain rhythm—for such an otherwise realistic painting the background doesn't seem to fit. I don't know. The figure is posed and stiff, while the curtain and sky are soft and billowing....
> —*Art teacher, grades 1-5, Springdale, Ark.*

At times, blogs revealed the participants' newfound insights about a work of art and their process of making connections between the art object and their own daily experiences as teachers and individuals. While this occurred in our in-person workshops, the blogs provided a space that was private and part of the teacher's daily lives, yet also part of the life of the museum—a curious combination that proved fertile for discovery in a distinctly different way from on-site workshops. In this excerpt, a teacher considers how a room might also be seen as a portrait after she explored a Web feature of the *Gubbio Studiolo*, an intarsia-paneled study from the Italian Renaissance:

> I have never considered a room, or a picture of a room, a portrait. I have never specifically thought about what the room tells you about the person who lives there, but this is such an obvious thing when you walk into rooms. When you would walk into my classroom, you immediately know what my students are lear-ning about, doing, and what is important to me as a teacher and them as students. When you walk into a child's bedroom, the posters/pictures they have, their decorations, choice of colors, organization, tells you so much about them as a person. I have never really thought of this as a portrait, and this particular work struck me....
>
> *—Elementary school deaf education specialist, Madison, Wisc.*

At other times the teachers' blogs became concrete lesson ideas that illustrated how they planned to adapt a work of art for their particular group of students. Rather than submitting a typical lesson plan or outline, a teacher from Dubai brainstorms about her encounter with a work of art explored in the workshop, the *Tughra of Sleyman the Magnificent*, and reveals her ideas for introducing it to her students:

> Because my students either speak Arabic or are learning Arabic, there are many fun activities that could be done with this work. We could create our own portraits in this style with the students' initials. With the help of the Arabic teacher, we could do this in

LIST OF COMPARATIVE QUESTIONS (please type below--do not erase list of similarities and differences further down in the wiki)

Questions from Liz S:
1. If you could step into one of these paitings which one would it be and why?

2. What do you thik is happening in each of these scenes? Do you thik the people are speaking with each other? What are they saying?

3. Which clothes would you like to wear?

4. Look closely, what is it like there/ how are the settings different from each other?

Comp. questions:
1.) If you were to create another panel-like a story board, for each of these works what would the next panel look like? What ∣ would you utilize?
2.) If you were to switch the backgrounds of the Stela and the Woman at the casement, how would you portray that scene ar it would affect the figures, how?
3.) Switching the figures in each work, so that the Woman in red is facing the seated Egyptian figure and the 2 smaller figures facing the man leaning in the window, what conversation would take place in each work? Cynthia M.

JESSICA   1. What do you think the writing in the Egyptian sculpture is saying? Why do you think this? Create a writt for the European painting. What would you write? Why? What style would you choose to write in? 2. What is the relationship ∣ the figures in each of the portraits? Why do you think this? 3. What do you think each of these portraits is made from? Why? you think the artists chose these specific materials? Inquiry Qs----Carolyn S

Fig. 1: Example of a wiki area in the Epsilen Global Learning System

English and in Arabic and then compare. The students could decide what information they want to include in a "picture" of who they are. We could discuss whether one "looks" more like them than the other. Since we do the typical "All About Me" unit at the beginning of the year, this would be a great collaborative project between my classroom and the Arabic classroom.
— *2nd grade teacher, Dubai, United Arab Emirates*

These blogs, which combined personal reflection and open dialogue, captured valuable information about our participants' thought processes and questions, about their experiences and how they might approach the works of art with their students. Further, because the blogs could be re-read or expanded, and because others could contribute comments to these blog entries, the conversations continued and deepened over days and weeks.

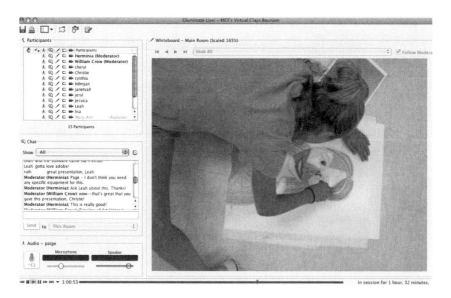

Fig 2: Image of virtual class reunion live webinar session in Elluminate Live, Nov. 14, 2007.

Wiki and Real-Time Interaction: Collaboration and Community Building

In our hyperlinked world there are many ways to connect visitors to the museum and to each other—social networking sites, e-newsletters, e-mail lists, and list-servs. Although these can be useful ways of maintaining communication, we found that the process of collaboration, and even conflict, builds community. During the workshop, as teachers worked in wikis to compile information, edited inquiry-based questions and jointly built a PowerPoint classroom resource, we found that they had interest and investment in the final outcome. The wiki tool allowed participants to constantly build upon each others' contributions in the spirit of improvement and bonded group members despite geographic distance or other differences. They communicated with one another— even beyond the final date of the workshop—in order to share additional information or ideas, and the museum and its collections were center-pieces of those conversations. Since the community of the workshop was not bound by the museum's walls, it was possible for the learning to sustain itself over a long period of time.

Perhaps the strongest evidence that the participants felt connected to a community of learners despite the geographic distance was a "virtual class reunion" that took place more than three months after the conclusion of the online workshop. During this live webinar session, participants were invited to create short PowerPoint presentations that showcased an activity they had developed and completed with their students based on a work of art that had been explored during the summer workshop. The teachers were very enthusiastic about this opportunity to continue to share ideas with their colleagues and show-case their students' achievements. It became a type of self-motivated and open-ended assessment that provided us with concrete examples of how teachers and students are using MMA-produced resources in their classrooms. Using synchronous webinar tools, the participants could instantly be brought back together, regardless of their physical locations, to demonstrate how they used our online museum resources.

Learning from Learners

The interactive qualities of blogs, wikis and real-time online communication have caused us to consider the impact of Web 2.0 tools on our in-person teacher workshops. Could these tools be employed to create a more blended (online and in-person) experience for our teachers, rather than isolating the museum-based and Web-based interactions? Could the reflective practice of blogging, collaborative wiki tools and live webinars expand and deepen the encounters that occur between teachers, museum educators and our collections? Further, noting that these processes unfold over days, weeks or months, should the format of our teacher programs change?

The process of creating and implementing the online teacher workshop has helped us see value in the multiplicity of museum experiences that may occur: online and in-person, synchronous and asynchronous, personal and public, individual and collective. We see the direction toward the learner-centric approach in museum education and the user-centric development of the Web as very compatible trends. As museum education has embraced interactive conversations with visitors, so has technology changed from Web "browsing" to the participatory culture of Web 2.0. As user-generated content expands to become the engine that powers the Web and as interactivity becomes the core of communication and education, we must consider how museums through their online resources and perhaps through a renewed approach to in-person programs can create deeper and more meaningful experiences with visitors.

ENDNOTES

1 See Falk and Dierking, *Learning in Museums*, chapter 3.

2 For more information about interactive videoconferencing, visit The Center for Interactive Learning and Collaboration at www.cilc.org.

3 See Stephen Weil, "From Being About Something to Being For Somebody," *Making Museums Matter*, Smithsonian Institution, Washington, DC, 2002.

4 Lev Vygotsky (1896-1934) was a pioneering developmental psychologist who studied child development and its relationship to cultural mediation and interpersonal communication, among other areas. Among this best-known works is *Mind and Society* (1930). John Dewey (1859-1952) was an American philosopher, psychologist and educational reformer known for his writings about the importance of educative experience. Among his many works is a key essay on aesthetics, *Art and Experience* (1934). Jean Piaget (1896-1980) was a Swiss philosopher, natural scientist and developmental theorist, well known for his work studying children and cognitive development. Among his major works is *The Origins of Intelligence in Children* (1953).

5 Gardner, H. *Frames of mind: The theory of multiple intelligences*. Basic Books, New York, 1983.

6 Falk, John H., and Dierking, Lynn D. Learning from Museums: *Visitor Experiences and the Making of Meaning*. Altamira Press, 2000.

7 Thomas L. Friedman, *The World is Flat*.

8 See details in *Open Source, Open Access: New Models for Museums*, in *The Digital Museum*, edited by Herminia Din and Phyllis Hecht, 2007.

9 See *The Work of Art in the Age of Mechanical Reproduction* by Walter Benjamin, 1935 and also Theodor Adorno and Max Horkheimer *The Culture Industry: Enlightenment as Mass Deception*, 1944.

10 For a discussion of the movement from a service economy to an "experience economy" in which consumers are seeking memorable and transformative experiences rather than services and products, see Joseph Pine II and James Gilmore's *The Experience Economy* (1999).

11 Epsilen is a new environment for learners and professionals that places social networking and ePortfolios at the center of eLearning, described by some users as an "Academic Facebook." www.epsilen.com

12 Elluminate Live is a Java-based software application that provides live e-Learning and Web collaboration. www.elluminate.com

CHAPTER 2

Getting Started

I go back to trying to breathe, slowly and calmly, and I finally notice the one-inch picture frame that I put on my desk to remind me of short assignments. It reminds me that all I have to do is to write down as much as I can see through a one-inch picture frame. This is all I have to bite off for the time being. All I am going to do right now, for example, is write that one paragraph that sets the story…

— *Bird by Bird* by Anne Lamott

Online learning environments, paired with the almost infinite resources of the Internet, offer an incredible array of possibilities for educational experiences. There exist vast amounts of resources, online "how to" discussions and demonstrations and a broad spectrum of digital tools—some well-established, others new and in development. However, this vast and ever-changing digital landscape is daunting for anyone interested in exploring the potential applications of online learning in the museum. A simple Internet search on the topic of online learning reveals thousands of potential avenues to explore. Where to begin? And what might work best and be most appropriate for a museum?

Museum professionals are already skilled in ways of inviting visitor participation and engagement. We understand that creativity and forging new territory is also about taking risks. Like any new endeavor, creating an online learning experience for museum visitors involves experimentation, practice and patience.

In her book *Bird by Bird*, author and educator Anne Lamott describes to her readers the genesis of the book's title. She narrates a story from childhood when her brother, overwhelmed by the prospect of writing a 20-page paper on the topic of birds, is stumped and frustrated by the prospect of such a seemingly insurmountable task. Their father, sympathetic to his son's situation, offers the useful advice to take it "bird by bird," or one step at a time. Perhaps the best starting point in the process of embarking in the world of online learning is to start with what you know, take things one step at a time and consider aspects of what you are already doing that could grow, deepen, expand or change.

While we emphasize that effective online learning is not about translating an onsite encounter, it is important to consider how existing and potential audiences could grow into an online community of learners. Could students in an offsite program participate in an online visit? Are there activities in the museum setting that could have a different dynamic if placed in an online environment as a component of the program? Consider how the museum staff currently interacts with its visitors and how the staff would like to interact with them. Are there conversations you wish you could have with your visitors? Online learning is not about translating experiences, but it can involve transferring to a new realm the communication and teaching skills that you already possess.

Only you, your colleagues and your intended audience can answer these questions. As educators and museums professionals know well, there is no magic formula that will work for every situation or institution. Nor is one approach instantly replicable and equally successful in another. The following chapter explores these issues and offers a starting point for the process of developing and using online learning in your museum.

THE MEANS

As we impart information, ask questions and involve visitors, we primarily rely on language—speaking to one another. We also utilize non-verbal forms of communication, such as gestures, visual cues, diagrams, maps or music. Many times we do this as second nature without considering how these communicative elements are essential in our teaching or in our daily lives.

In the field of online teaching and learning, there are similar ways of communicating, but often these exchanges are compressed and occur through computer-media means. Both educators and learners may exchange information and ideas through the online environment using text and even audio, video and live conversation. However, in many ways the in-person environment of the museum and the online environment of the computer are different. An educator may never see the students. The interaction may occur asynchronously or with learners logging on at their own convenience or schedule. It can be more difficult to notice visual cues and body language, since learners are expressing themselves through other means.

There are a number of tools museums might consider in communicating and interacting with online learners. While these tools are constantly evolving, the following section describes some of the most commonly used, with examples of each.

Asynchronous Tools

Users may access these tools at any given time. Participants are not required to be online at the same time in order to engage in this Web-based activity. Participants contribute to the interaction on their own schedule, rather than at a specific time.

• **Threaded Discussion:** an electronic forum created by individuals and connected via an electronic network in which messages or postings are grouped according to topic threads. Sometimes these are found as tools embedded within larger Course Management Systems (CMS).

- **Blog (weblog):** a dynamic online publishing system designed for two-way interaction by posting narratives and receiving responsive commentary. Examples: Blogger, Wordpress, LiveJournal.

- **Wiki:** an online tool enabling users to add, remove, edit and change content remotely and collaboratively. Examples: pbwiki, Google Docs, Wikipedia.

- **Podcast/Vodcast (video podcast):** a digital media file that is distributed by subscription (paid or unpaid) over the Internet for playback on mobile devices and/or personal computers. Examples: Audacity, iTunes.

- **Online Group and Social Networking:** a Web-based networking service that focuses on building online communities of people who share interests and/or activities, or who want to explore the interests and activities of others. Examples: MySpace, Facebook, Yahoo Groups, Twitter, Ning.

- **Online Media Aggregating and Sharing:** a website where users can upload, view and share different types of digital files such as videos, music, PowerPoint presentations, photos, etc. Examples: YouTube, Slide Share, Flickr, iTune, Voicethread.

- **Course Management System (CMS):** a collection of software tools providing an online environment for course interactions that typically include a variety of online tools and environments such as digital drop boxes for posting learning materials, a grade book, integrated email tool, chat room, threaded discussion board, wiki, etc. Examples: Moodle, Angel Learning, Epsilen, Blackboard/WebCT, Sakai.

Synchronous Tools

These tools allow participants to meet online on a given date and time to communicate and exchange ideas between two or more people over the Internet, so that they may interact with one another in real time.

- **Webinar software or services:** a web-based conferencing tool used to conduct live, collaborative and interactive, real-time meetings or presentations via the Internet. Examples: Adobe Connect, Elluminate Live, Microsoft Live, WebEx, Skype, GotoMeeting, Wimba.

• **Chat (online):** a type of synchronous text messaging that instantly exchanges messages through an application via the Internet. Examples: Instant Message, Skype, Yahoo Chat.

After researching these possibilities, museums are still faced with another challenge. Which of these tools would be most effective for a particular program idea, learning situation or group of individuals? When should we use a particular approach, and to what extent? In the following scenarios, we will examine some situations where online learning could provide opportunities for deeper engagement.

SOME POSSIBILITIES: THREE SCENARIOS

A common myth about the use of technology is that one can just pick up the tool and "plug it in" to almost any situation. While we understand and encourage experimentation and pilot projects, it is essential to consider the reasons why you are using a particular medium with a particular audience. Just as one would consider content, pedagogy and ways of engaging your visitors in-person, online learning has its own set of considerations and challenges. Imagine yourself in the following fictional scenarios. What possibilities might online learning offer museum professionals and visitors in these situations?[22]

Situation I:

You work in a small historic house that has a diverse collection of decorative arts, furniture and costumes from the 18th century. In addition to the collection, perhaps one of the greatest assets of the historic house are the stories about the family that used to live here and what life was like in the late 1700s. You have also noticed that many visitors who go on your regular tours of the house make comparisons between their daily lives and the lifestyles of the 18th century. They enjoy seeing the similarities and differences between objects in the house and objects that they themselves use daily.

Possible Online Learning Opportunities:

• A blog that includes comparisons between objects in the collection and their contemporary counterparts, with images and multimedia and opportunities for readers to share their own comments and ideas.

• A podcast that narrates stories about the family that used to live in the house, with opportunities for visitors to record and share their own stories.

• A live chat or webinar during which a museum educator, using first-person interpretation in a question-and-answer format, interacts with visitors in real time.

Situation II:

You work for a contemporary art center that exhibits the newest and most challenging works created by both local and internationally known artists. The special exhibitions change about three times a year and usually include art in non-traditional formats: installation, performance and time-based works such as video and projections. Many of the artists who have exhibited at your museum have been willing to speak in public programs, all of which have been digitally recorded in both audio and video. The museum building itself is a work of art, having dynamic and dramatic angles, unique building materials and views of the city. You have found that many visitors come specifically to see the building and often spend quite a bit of time exploring the architecture rather than exploring the works of art on view in the exhibitions.

Possible Online Learning Opportunities:

Offer to high school art teachers a three-week, online threaded discussion about a particular artist's work. Include the participation of the artist and links to videos of the artist's performances that have been recently uploaded to the Web. Invite the participating teachers to brainstorm online about possible classroom teaching applications.

After working in the museum with a group of college students studying architecture, create a mock architecture competition for the design of a new, expanded building. Have students share their original designs for a new museum on a wiki site, so that everyone can add their comments and ideas.

Working across museum departments and with the assistance of a talented intern, create a blog about the installation process of an artist's work in the galleries. Link this to the exhibition information on the website. Invite comments and questions from visitors and incorporate the information from the blog into an in-person series of talks about the exhibition.

Situation III:

You work at a children's museum in a mid-sized city. While your museum has a wide range of exhibits and programs designed for families, you have noticed that your attendance is quite low except for two annual "Family Day" celebrations on weekends when attendance peaks. Recently you received feedback from families, praising the family guides that include activities that parents and children can complete during their visit; these are available for free download from your website. You have also heard from several parents on your Advisory Board that it would be helpful to offer some type of orientation workshop for parents, so that they might have more suggested activities to do with their children during their visit. However, they were also quick to point out that many parents work full-time and it is difficult for them to travel to the museum after work on weekdays.

Possible Online Learning Opportunities:

● Offer a live webinar or chat session for parents on a Thursday evening, modeling a variety of activities that they can do with their children during their weekend visit.

● Create a podcast or vodcast (with video) for children and families, along with an online discussion forum to answer their questions and spark ideas for their visit.

• Invite a small group of parents, including some on your Advisory Board, to contribute to an online threaded discussion about how the museum could improve its family guides and online resources.

Perhaps one or more of the above scenarios sound familiar to you or are directly applicable to your current situation. They might prompt an idea that could be a potential fit for your museum and visitors. The scenarios described above are brainstorming exercises, and one would need more information about each museum's mission and priorities before undertaking any online learning project. The following steps introduce ways for museums to shape initial ideas into programs.

SOME STEPS TOWARD REFLECTING VALUES IN ONLINE LEARNING CHOICES

A. Consider Your Institution, Your Visitors and Yourself

Before initiating an online learning project, consider how it will contribute to the mission of your institution. How does it connect with existing resources, including staff, as well as the current priorities for the organization? Does this online learning opportunity advance the museum's existing goals and objectives? To what extent is your institution uniquely poised to contribute in this area?

When creating any type of learning experience, it is advantageous to think of the participants and the outcomes. What do you want the learners to take away from this experience? Will you provide the learners with an incentive to enroll or participate? Consider what motivates your existing museum visitors to come for programs. Do teachers receive materials they can use with students? Do they have opportunities to interact with museum staff or guest speakers? Do they receive graduate credit or receive a certificate of participation that they can take back to their school? Will you offer the program for a fee?

Finally, consider your own time, energy and current skills. How much time and commitment are you asking of yourself and your colleagues?

What kinds of skills and expertise do you currently have and which do you need to acquire? Bear in mind that in addition to building technical skills using new digital tools, it is even more important to have other types of writing and presentation skills for delivering effective online learning experiences. The level of skill required will vary depending on the outcome desired. For example, if you are creating a simple blog, it will require a high degree of writing or narration skills but relatively few technical skills. Conversely, a podcast that captures visitor feedback may require little museum-produced content but will require a high degree of audio production to record and edit.

B. Take Stock of Your Resources

Part of developing an online learning project requires examining resources. Consider existing materials that could be incorporated into an online learning program, such as teacher materials, podcasts, video or images. How many of these items exist in a digital format? If they do not, what steps are necessary to create or re-format these materials? Are any of them already on the museum's website and what are the possibilities for teaching with these materials, rather than merely inviting web visitors to download them?

Another valuable resource is your colleagues. Seek out collaborators in your institution who are interested in online learning projects and those who have skills or content expertise. Start a conversation with your audio guide partners. You may find that there are staff members in your museum who are already teaching online for a university, write for a blog or online journal or have expertise producing videos or audio for the Web.

The process of seeking collaborators should also include research into potential funding sources for online learning projects. Numerous foundations, corporations and government grants earmark monies specifically for technology-related educational programs. Work closely with the museum's development or fundraising staff and seek their expertise.

C. Scope and Structure: The Internet and Instructional Design

As we consider the needs of our visitors, analyze and develop the content and implement and evaluate the program, we are effectively engaging in a process of instructional design. Although this is an extensive field of professional study, it is useful to consider some of the basic tenets of the much-used ADDIE model, an acronym that stands for the following five phases:

Analyze - analyze learner characteristics, task to be learned, etc.

Design - develop learning objectives, choose an instructional approach

Develop - create instructional or training materials

Implement - deliver or distribute the instructional materials

Evaluate - make sure the materials achieve the desired goals

Consider what the scope of this online learning experience will be. Will it involve 15 people or 50? Will it be a live webinar that lasts an hour, a week-long threaded discussion or a three-week intensive? Again, it is often useful to start small when embarking on a project. Remember that staff interaction with participants is only the proverbial tip of the iceberg, since the development of program activities and content may require days, weeks or months before the online experience begins.

Regardless of the communication tools you decide to use, the length of the encounter or participants involved, be sure you are selecting methods and platforms that are as user-friendly as possible—both for museum staff and for your visitors. Online learning environments should be developed that are easy to navigate, aesthetically pleasing and as intuitive as possible.

In an online learning experience, users are instantly connected through the Internet to many different resources, including your own museum's website. Consider such advantages and think how participants will make use of your existing website and online resources. Connect with other online resources when needed and appropriate. Finally, when outlining a possible online learning experience, consider whether you will offer an in-person component at the museum. You may also want to consider other options, especially for participants from distant locations, such as mailing the participants passes or tickets to visit the museum whenever they are able.

Online environments, in particular comprehensive course management systems, have been developed primarily for learning that includes a formal structure and curriculum. Higher education and increasingly K-12 schools have used these online portals to include lesson plans, formal sets of activities and semester-long credit courses. For museums, it is important to consider how online learning offered by museums would, or should, differ from online learning offered in school or university environments. Author and educator David Carr suggests that museums and libraries would be best served if they placed a sign above their doors reading "This is not a school."[4] While some of the terminology and structures that exist with digital educational tools may call a program a "class," or a "course," or identify components as "lessons," consider how your work might be similar or different.

As you begin to design the online educational program and the tools and approaches that will be used, be aware that digital tools offer diverse ways of interacting that can be useful for different types of activities and encounters. Below are some examples that you may want to consider.

Asynchronous Design
Pre-Program Orientation Activities:
- Participants receive pre-program materials, either digitally or by mail.
- During an introductory week online, participants create their online account, write a blog entry introducing themselves and get acquainted with the online environment.
- Participants contribute to a threaded discussion, responding to a central question or idea that will be explored during the online program.

Individual Activities:
- Participants complete online questionnaires about their prior experience and skills that connect with the program content.
- Participants use blogs as a means to record about their experience online.
- Offline, participants create a hands-on project, visit a local museum or interview someone local about the program content, and then upload and share these experiences with the group.

Group Activities:
- Participants contribute to threaded discussions. A conversation builds over days or weeks.
- Groups collaborate on projects, compile information and edit and share information in wikis and shareable documents.

Synchronous Design
- Participants discuss content in real time.
- The group collectively brainstorms and shares information spontaneously.
- Educators and participants can lead guided tours of websites.
- Virtual break-out rooms can group participants for live interaction.
- Guest speakers can be brought into the program for question and answer sessions.

Blended Design
- As a component of the online experience, participants are invited to attend an on-site program at the museum and meet face-to-face.
- The on-site experience may occur at the beginning, middle or end of the online learning component.

D. Assessment and Reflection as an Ongoing Process: Seeing Evidence of Success

Like all museum programming, online programming also includes assessment as an essential component that must be considered. While it is beyond the scope of this book to outline all of the methodologies and concepts that are useful for museum program evaluation, you will want to consider what success will look like at the conclusion of this online learning program. Pinpoint one, two or three main ideas that you would ideally like the learner to walk away with at the conclusion of the program. Ask what evidence of this learning would be acceptable to you, the institution and your supporters.

Documentation of ideas, discussions and activities can be easily captured by technology. Because participants post their thoughts and questions at each step, it is possible to observe how they are interacting with the program content and the instructors at each stage. This is also useful for summative evaluation at the conclusion of the program. Since online learning programs may take place over the course of several days or weeks, it is possible to use this ongoing feedback to make improvements to the program as it continues.

While many museums are now actively using online tools for assessment, specifically online pre- and post-program surveys and questionnaires, digital assessment may take many forms. Some of these include:

• **Reflective Blog Entries:** Participants blog about their experience in the program, either by responding to a directed question or open-ended approaches.

• **Virtual Class Reunions:** Using synchronous technology, participants are brought back together weeks, months or even years after the conclusion of a program so that they may share what they learned and provide concrete examples of how they have applied the learning experience

• **Concept Mapping:** Using online concept mapping tools, participants may draw diagrams that express their current thinking, and then add to these digital drawings at the conclusion of the program[5]

• **Multimedia Commentary:** Using audio, video or text, participants can comment on screenshots from the program, photographs and diagrams in order to provide feedback.[6]

E. Planning for Progress and Sustainability

The start of most new projects presents some challenges. However, take time to explore the horizon and reflect on how the program will progress, change, expand or be sustained in the future after the initial pilot. Will you, your colleagues and your visitors have the time and resources to be engaged in future online learning opportunities? Should the programs be free or fee-based to contribute to their sustainability? As you create this initial project, be sure to document every aspect well so that, if successful, a proposal might be crafted to a potential donor who would support more of these endeavors.

Once an online learning project has proven successful in your institution, but sure to make time to reflect on the experience, discuss the potential for building on this foundation and how it might be improved in the future. Consider other collaborators who might join future programs, both internal and external to the museum, and how these new partners may enhance the online experience as well as anchor this endeavor in the institution.

Starting a Blog

Conceptualizing, designing, implementing and evaluating an online learning experience with visitors can be a time-consuming, a complex and challenging process. As with any worthwhile collaborative effort, there are obstacles, conflicts and setbacks. However, the rewarding learning possibilities that online interaction can offer museums merit time, hard work and patience. In the following case study, Jennifer Rothman, associate vice president for Children's and Public Education, describes how the New York Botanical Garden began their first blog, and some of the challenges and rewards that resulted.

The New York Botanical Garden is a 117-year old institution. With that come standards, styles and procedures that have been honed and perfected and then honed and perfected again. In keeping with these high standards, a typical publication is not released to the public until many rounds of editing and revision have occurred and the piece is a perfect representation of the Botanical Garden's style, mission and ideals.

A blog does not live well in those confines.

A blog has standards, styles and procedures all its own.

Despite this major hurdle, *Plant Talk* was launched in June of 2008; but conversations about the format, content, process and maintenance began no less then a year prior, and probably much sooner than that. The blog seed had been simultaneously planted in several departments well before *Plant Talk* was launched. The scientists wanted to post about their work, the public relations team saw it as a good communications tool, education (my area) naturally saw it as an educational tool and the Web team saw it as a natural progression of our ever improving website. Luckily, a few of us started talking to each other and we began to con-ceptualize a site that would fit all of our needs. The initial team consisted of me, the director of the website, and the manager of public relations.

Our conversation began with identifying our audience and our goals. After much back and forth, we ultimately decided that our audience would be the general visitor and that our goal would be to provide a behind-the-scenes look at all aspects of the Garden—including science, horticulture and gardening—as written by the Garden staff itself. I think we each wanted to be more specific, both in goals and audience. For example, I would have liked to narrow the audience to the home gardener, the family audience or teachers. But for the first effort we all agreed that we would have more success getting buy-in from all departments and approval to launch if we targeted a wider audience.

The next step was to brainstorm ideas for content and figure out how to keep the blog updated regularly, ideally every weekday, with existing staff and without a dedicated blog writer. As blog readers ourselves, the working group discussed what blogs kept us coming back and why. We enjoyed blogs that were updated daily or every other day at the longest. The tone that drew us in was authoritative, well written and edited, casual and conversational and a bit voyeuristic.

The Garden had a history of authoritative, well crafted writing, but the rest would be a departure from our typical publications. Knowing that this new format and style might be a tough sell to others at the Garden, we embarked on creating a process and procedure that would convince them that the site would maintain a level of integrity fitting of the Garden. If we were to achieve the desired tone, content and regularity of posting, it meant that we needed to get others onboard.

First, our working team embarked on creating a calendar of topics. We listed Monday through Friday along the x-axis and weeks one through four on the y-axis. We then filled in each slot with a potential post. For example, on every Friday of the month we would always have a post about the weekend programming and on Tuesdays we would feature a gardening tip. On a few of the slots we decided to feature a photo of what's in bloom, a curator's choice post on another and various other ideas to scatter throughout.

Once we had our calendar mapped out we embarked on finding content we could repurpose. The more information we already had, the less writing we would need to solicit from others. Luckily, we have an abundance of tip sheets from a long-running home gardening program and a library chock full of horticulture, gardening and science nformation, much of it written by Garden staff. Of course all of these resources were edited in the formal style that the Garden had perfected.

Sorting through this material and the calendar, we discussed the workload for different individuals and how that work would be distributed throughout the year. For example, we thought that our Gardener for Public Education could re-edit all of the Tuesday's Tips for the year in advance and that we needed only one post from a curator each month (since we have many curators). Our goal was to convince others that the writing commitment would be minimal.

At this point, we brought the Garden's Editorial Director onto our working team. It was crucial that we have her support since we were at once adding to her workload and also suggesting that we break style and (gasp!) publish posts that the editorial team may not review.

She helped us to identify how we could re-edit materials and provided editing basics and garden writing styles that had to be followed. Her confidence in the project would help others approve the blog.

At this point, we decided that we needed just enough approval to move on and were very careful about showing the calendar and proposal to others. Though we certainly welcomed creativity and ideas, we would not seek advice or guidance from a larger contingent until we had more to work with. We were afraid that too many ideas could have an adverse effect on moving forward. We showed these select individuals how much of the information already existed and that we could distribute writing assignments among their staff. Though today the calendar isn't strictly followed, it helped us show that the blog was achievable. We had also prepared a set of goals for the blog that provided the rationale for the blog's existence; this helped us to explain why we were starting the blog and what we hoped to achieve.

With enough buy-in to move forward and a few adjustments to our calendar based on feedback, we set about developing a month's worth of content. This is what we would show to a wider audience. The web designer used a public blogging tool that he custom-designed to have a similar aesthetic to other pages of our web site. Content was repurposed and edited and new content and images were created.

This initial month was first shown to the editorial director and was met with some criticism. Although the new, more casual tone was accepted there were stylistic elements that couldn't be ignored. For example, we always capitalize the "T" in "The" before our name but had not done so on the blog. The month of content was edited and then finally shown to the president of the Garden and to other stakeholders, including the heads of the science, horticulture and education departments. From there, we were given the go-ahead to continue. We had achieved the approval we were looking for and were ready to launch. *Plant Talk* officially went live.

By this time, the working group had been expanded beyond the initial three. It now included the interpretation specialist from the Education Department, a web designer, an editor and a PR associate. The expanded team would have ultimate say over what would be published and would be responsible for brainstorming topics, soliciting writers and editing and publishing posts. After a few contributions for the blog that were off-tone and not in keeping with the blog's goal, the group decided to create writer's guidelines. All contributors would be given this guide and the working team would use the guide to edit posts before publishing.

This group began by creating a mission statement:

> The mission of The New York Botanical Garden's blog is to present original, experience-based information that reflects the breadth of goings-on at the Garden with a behind-the-scenes perspective from staff, volunteers and students that cannot be found elsewhere. These insider views complement existing communications vehicles such as the visitor Web site, e-notes, Garden News, and press releases, with the purpose of stimulating Garden fans and attracting new audiences.

The guidelines also urged contributors to write posts that were original, written from a personal experience point of view and easily under-standable for the layperson. The posts should be fun and timely, with information not found on the visitor Web site. They needed to be accu-rate, consistent with the Garden's blog style and standard (examples were provided) and no longer than 400 words. It was suggested that the post be accompanied by an image, video or sound clip (with usage rights from the copyright owner and model releases if people are in the photo). Each post was to be accompanied by a tagline with the author's name and affiliation to the Garden.

Way back at the start of the conversation, the initial team maintained that the blog would be a one-way communication tool. We would not allow comments. The reasoning was that blogging was so new to so many people at the Garden that allowing visitors to contribute might be deemed dangerous and we were afraid it would impede the progress of approval. I still think this was a good idea when seeking approval. But after strong urging from summer college interns who convinced us that a blog wasn't much of a blog without comments, we began allowing comments soon after launching. Since then, we have not had to remove a single comment. These same interns were savvy about viral marketing and helped us to update and expand our pages on MySpace, Facebook and Flickr and added widgets and other tools to our site. This has surely helped build our readership.

At this writing the blog has been in operation for about 6 months. Although the roots of the project hold it firmly in place, it has blossomed into a spectacular new and unexpected medium with which to reach and interact with our audience. The initial calendar is no longer followed, although the Tuesday Tips and the Friday listing of weekend programs survived the many changes. We have had over 13,000 unique visitors and nearly 45,000 page reads. We measure our success in readership, through our comments section and by other blogs and Web sites linking to *Plant Talk* and mentioning it to their own readers. With minimal publicity or marketing, *Plant Talk* is already creating a buzz in the blogosphere, recognized as one of the pre-eminent institutional blogs of its kind.

The content team continues to meet regularly to discuss and plan future entries and also to make sure that the blog stays true to its mission. The biggest struggle seems to be keeping it from becoming a promotional or marketing tool. Sometimes the team also has difficulty soliciting writers, although just about every department has contributed ideas and entries.

Blogging really is as easy and free as the free services (such as Blogger and Typepad) say it is. And you literally can create a blog, write and publish a post in a matter of minutes. A blog's success, however, is directly proportionate to the amount of pre-planning and commitment one has to maintaining it. So although there is no actual cost to publishing, the cost of a successful blog will be realized in hours of staff time and effort. The net result is a new outlet for information, conversation, communication and a new online audience. By the time this case study is printed, I can all but guarantee that *Plant Talk* will be different and more effective in ways that I never imagined.

ENDNOTES

1 From *Bird by Bird: Some Instructions on Writing and Life* by Anne Lamott. Anchor Books/Doubleday, New York, 1994.

2 The following fictional scenarios were drafted by the authors and originally used during a technology-related program offered by the New York City Museum Educators Roundtable (NYCMER) on Saturday, November 22, 2008 at the Metropolitan Museum of Art. Participants at the session helped to brainstorm the potential online learning solutions presented.

3 The origins of the ADDIE model are debated. For more information about instructional design and models that incorporate and build upon the ADDIE model, see Dick, W., & Carey, L.(1978). *The Systematic Design of Instruction*. Glenview, IL.: Scott, Foresman.

4 See David Carr's *The Promise of Cultural Institutions*, 2003.

5 Some current examples of this type of tool are www.inspiration.com and www.mindmeister.com

6 A tool that we have been using for gathering commentary about media is www.voicethread.com

CHAPTER 3

Blurred Boundaries: Museums Unfixed in Place and Time

A fter traveling for several hours on a crowded bus one chilly
morning in early April, a group of high school students enters
the recently renovated Visitor Center of Gettysburg National
Park. They see articles and artifacts from the Civil War: Union
and Confederate soldiers' uniforms, a wall of rifles and a display
of flags from the period. They move through the galleries, stopping from
time to time to listen to a guide who explains the history of the Civil War.
They ask some questions and spend time looking closely at the objects
on view. After about an hour in the Visitor Center, they walk outside and
move to the Cyclorama, an immersive, multi-media display that tells the
story of the Battle of Gettysburg through narrative, dioramas, lights and
special effects. As the group moves outside, they notice the air has started
to warm from the sun, and the fog that had settled in that morning has
started to clear. They look out toward the rolling hills and see the landscape, birds flying overhead and they notice the quiet. They take a short
bus ride away from the Visitors Center and step onto the ground. The
wet morning dew is on the grass. One student asks the guide, "So is this
the place?" and the guide responds, "Yes, this is it. Below our feet is the
ground where thousands of soldiers died in 1864 during the largest battle
ever fought on American soil."

A few hundred miles east of Gettysburg, a group of 10 adult visitors
considers what it would have been like to live in a 350-square foot
apartment on New York City's Lower East Side in the 1860s.

Surrounded by the hubbub of rapidly growing communities of recently arrived immigrants, families were fortunate to find any kind of housing in the land of opportunity. They arrived to find challenges that are difficult to fathom today. Families of four, six or even eight would inhabit small cramped quarters, use a common outhouse behind the building or, if they were lucky, a toilet in the hallway. They would cautiously live and work to avoid the ever-present danger of fire and disease. Today, the Lower East Side Tenement Museum invites visitors to experience these living quarters in a variety of first-person interpretative programs and conversations and is very much about the location and experience of walking through these living quarters.

WHERE IS THE MUSEUM?

Typically, museums can draw strength from their physical places. Sometimes this is an actual historic site where an event happened, or a unique environment that can be examined with both a historical and contemporary lens. The smell, size and scale and ambience of a place can greatly expand our understanding of a museum and of the objects themselves. Further, experiencing both the physical and cultural landscape of a physical place can deepen our understanding of location, objects, history, even ourselves. What was it like to walk across the landscape of Pennsylvania in the 1860s? How do the rolling hills, the trees and the sweet smell of the grass inform our understanding of this location? What would it have been like to live in New York City's Lower East Side in the same period and how is that neighborhood similar or different today?

The physical location of a museum can be one of its greatest assets but also one of its greatest challenges. How many of us would love to visit the Adirondack Museum in the mountains of New York State, or Frank Lloyd Wright's Fallingwater House? But alas, we do not have plans to travel to the mountains when the Adirondack Museum is open (seasonally), nor can we visit rural western Pennsylvania to see the Wright architectural masterpiece. How many times have we heard the laments of museum professionals as they exclaim "our visitors can't find us," or "since we're out in the boondocks we don't get many visitors." Even urban institutions complain, "Parking is such a nightmare that visitors don't want to come in."

At times, place can be arbitrary in the museum context. Consider the times when you have toured a site that has been moved or rebuilt, visited a museum that now lives in a brand new building downtown or enjoyed a rural museum that is off the beaten path. How much of your museum experience was essential to that particular place? As we stand in front of a painting or sculpture, we hear lectures and information in the realms of biography, history or context—important items to consider but often not critical to our specific time and place. How connected are we, in the moment of learning, to our physical surroundings?[1]

All of these questions can be debated. Ideally of course we would like to have our visitors physically with us as much as possible. At the core, this is a question of uniqueness: What are the special qualities of our museums that must be experienced and contemplated onsite, within the walls of the museum building, and how do those experiences relate to the visitors?[2] At the same time, museums are uniquely poised to facilitate different types of experiences that can occur offsite or online. Those can be powerful and meaningful too for visitors and still aligned with a museum's vision and mission.

Place-based education, a rising field that has its roots in environmental and ecological education, theorizes that learners connect best to subjects and topics grounded in their own daily lives, experiences and communities.[3] Rather than discussing national or global issues in an abstract, textbook-centric way, advocates of place-based education posit that learners should learn about their own surroundings, their community members and their environments first-hand in order to have deep, personal experiences. In *The School and Society*, John Dewey advocated an experiential approach to student learning in the local environment: "Experience [outside the school] has its geographical aspect, its artistic and its literary, its scientific and its historical sides. All studies arise from aspects of the one earth and the one life lived upon it."[4] Dewey understood the power of place in creating meaningful educative experiences.

The core notion of place is the relationship between specificity and universal.In specificity, it is about the unique qualities of the museum object, the character of the site, the experiential qualities of the location; and in the universal, it is how these connect with the visitor's daily life, how they are relevant, what kinds of essential questions or universal themes are discovered. What does it mean to have a *localized* experience? How much of our own experiences that originate outside the physical location of the museum connect with our experiences inside the museum?

If we ask our visitors to reflect on topics that draw upon their own unique and personal backgrounds, digital environments provide a rich way to do it. Online learning can serve as a bridge between these worlds and help museums expand their boundaries.

WHERE ARE YOUR VISITORS?

When considering the unique qualities of your institution, or aspects of the learning that happens within the building, a key element to consider is, of course, your visitors. One should ask not only who these visitors are, but also where they are. Visitors may be local or regional, or visiting from abroad. Spend time examining who is currently entering the museum, which groups might be underserved or who the potential audience might be. The field of marketing has embraced this question, and museum marketing staffs have been eager to utilize blogging and online features in an effort to expand the museum's presence to a variety of publics. There may be individuals, groups or communities that you would like to reach in your educational endeavors that in the past have been limited to physical location. Perhaps the museum should offer more statewide programs for teachers who could benefit from professional development provided by the institution. Adult learners from across the country or across the globe could take advantage of a series of scholarly talks hosted by your institution and contribute to the dialogue. Students who are studying a topic that strongly connects with the museum would greatly benefit from an educational experience but are often faced with the limitations of the school day or travel costs.

The idea of a virtual visit, or a distance experience, has been around for some time. For well over two decades, museums have utilized videoconferencing as a potential solution. At first these programs were a means to essentially broadcast content to the learners, but recently they have become more interactive, with educators and presenters using inquiry-based approaches and document cameras to enliven the experience. However, while videoconferencing has its strength in bridging distance, both the content provider and the end-users must possess specialized equipment in order to connect with one another. While some schools have invested in videoconferencing technologies and even earmarked substantial funds to support student learning in this arena, the challenges of the equipment remain.

Besides the issues of physical place in the question "Where are your visitors?" one should also consider the more metaphorical level of the question. Where are your visitors in terms of their preparedness to try new online learning as a means to engage with the museum? This means access to computers and the Internet, but also their psychographic readiness to try this type of learning as a means to experience the museum. While sometimes museums make the erroneous assumption that only students and teens are interested in technology, online communication has become a lifeline for senior citizens, families who live in rural settings and individuals with disabilities. We should also consider the different levels of engagement that are needed for different types of visitors. An online learning program for seasoned, regular visitors would include different types of interactions and information from one offered to the novice museum visitor.

Finally, it is necessary to examine our own relationship to the museum and to an online learning endeavor. Does the museum staff work onsite at the building or are there staff members who work part-time or even at an offsite location? How could we benefit from involving educators or guest speakers from other locations or institutions? Beyond the considerations of physical location, is our current museum staff ready to undertake an experimental project in online education?

WHEN ARE YOU AND YOUR VISITORS AVAILABLE?

After considering where museum visitors and staff are, one might consider an equally important facet: When are museum visitors and staff available? As museum visitors attend programs during their leisure time, evenings, weekends, even holidays, museum staff must also be present for these programs. Beyond the traditional 9-5 workday, staff often arrange and re-arrange schedules in order to be present for our visitors. Online learning can push the issue of scheduling and workday into a different terrain because of the high degree of flexibility, at times liberating the museum professional from traditional scheduling confines.

Today a typical routine for a museum professional might include checking e-mail in the morning and responding to questions about a particular program or event. Later in the day, we interact with that same person by phone, conduct a program with a group in the galleries, and then in the afternoon see colleagues in a group meeting. At the end of the day as we leave the office for an appointment, we might add to a conversation that we began in the morning on our mobile device with a few questions to be discussed later in the week. At the end of the evening, we check e-mail again, or add to an online document that the group has created to brainstorm the project.

While this is typical for our work lives, we see a similar pattern in our personal lives. We continue conversations over time and over media, often in bits or short passages, and we continue to revisit them. We check in, we move on to another activity and then return to it. While much has been made about the deluge of work and entanglements that e-mail can cause, and multi-tasking skills have become a new requirement for our work style, it is clear that we and our visitors are learning how to communicate in different ways and over different amounts of time.

At first glance, one might question such a seemingly fragmented museum experience. What about an extended encounter with a museum object that lasts 20 or 30 minutes or even longer than an hour? Some museum visitors and educators proclaim that these types of extended experiences are ideal for moments of personal and collective discovery, or perhaps should be the sole focus of museum education. However, we also see that museum visitors learn over time, and sometimes are not even aware of what has been learned until long after the onsite visit to the museum. One might consider the example provided by John Falk and Lynn Dierking. In their seminal work *Learning from Museums*, they describe the experience of two young women who visited a Natural History Museum exhibition. While they both visited the same exhibition, they recalled different types and amounts of information. When the researchers followed up with these museum goers several months later, they had connected their learning to other experiences in their lives, and deepened their understanding.[5]

A challenge that we must consider is not only how and where we work, but also when we work with our visitors and with one another. As we enter into online conversations and activities with visitors, we may need to shift our schedules to meet the needs of these learners. However, this may also be an opportunity to release from the confines of a traditional schedule. We will need to reconsider what a program format might look like as it unfolds over several days or weeks online. Although this can prove to be one of the most non-traditional aspects of online learning, it also offers new and potentially rewarding ways to engage with our visitors.

TEACHING OVER TIME

In a typical museum-based education program, visitors are welcomed, enter the galleries, spend about an hour together, then continue their visit on their own or leave. In online teaching and learning, the experience may last an hour, or several, or may unfold over a period of days, weeks or months. Participants may have an intensive, live experience for only 60 minutes or a more intermittent, informal exchange over 60 days. As learners log on either simultaneously or on their own schedules, different types of interaction can unfold. Let us examine the three primary approaches to online teaching and learning: synchronous, asynchronous and blended, and see how these might affect museum education practice.

A. Spontaneity and Responsiveness in Synchronous Interaction

Synchronous interaction in an online environment occurs when all participants are online simultaneously. This happens through chat, instant messaging, live webinar technology or other means. The educator (sometimes called the moderator in synchronous environments) and participants may hear and see one another through webcams and microphones, but may also utilize a number of interactive multimedia tools such as file sharing, whiteboards and virtual breakout rooms.

Similar to an onsite, in-person experience, the strength of the synchronous experience is spontaneous interaction and the opportunity respond to ideas and questions in real time. The educator is placed in the role of "moderator" and participants may interact in real time, developing bonds and cohesion similar to those that occur in a physical setting. While some of the approaches and pedagogies of synchronous online learning are different from in-person teaching, educators are faced with many of the same issues that occur in a typical onsite museum program. These include balancing conversations so that many voices can be heard, keeping the session interactive (drawing, writing and multimedia aspects can be incorporated into these platforms) and ensuring that all participants feel welcomed, respected and safe.[6]

Synchronous sessions are convenient for the participants because interaction occurs on their "turf"—at home or wherever they have access to a computer and the Internet. While museums want visitors to enter their physical doorways, we should not undervalue this aspect of outreach and of dissolving barriers through live interaction with a museum's staff. In a sense, the museum can be in the homes and daily lives of the visitors in an active and engaging way.

B. Depth and Reflection in Asynchronous Interaction

In asynchronous interaction, the educator and the participants are online at different times, and participants can complete activities and add to conversations when they are able. As participants contribute to threaded discussion, blogs or collaborative wiki projects, they work at a pace that follows their own time and schedules. This is not to say that participants or educators can log on infrequently or haphazardly with different degrees of intensity and have the same outcome. Asynchronous interaction has a set of parameters that are established by an educator in advance. Depending on the scope of the program, participants may be asked to log in once a day, every 48 hours or only 2 or 3 times per week. Expectations are established from the outset.

Because the interaction may unfold and progress over a series of days or weeks, rather than seconds or minutes in a live situation, both educators and participants have a different relationship to the encounter. As threaded discussions are built and blog entries drafted, both the educator and the participants can take time to consider and craft their contributions in ways that are different from a typical onsite program. After doing some initial research, one might add information, links and multimedia to a conversation. Other participants might use their blogs as personal, reflective journals about their experiences in the program over several weeks.

This opportunity to gather one's thoughts can fundamentally change the nature of the conversations that happen in the online environment. Often participants will contribute information about their daily lives and how a current event connects with a topic that is being discussed online. They might post photographs and links to useful resources, or create and share a document that makes their point more effectively than would a text entry or even verbal exchange.

Another characteristic of asynchronous online learning is its cumulative nature. As wikis are built and edited, as lists of web links are posted and shared, all of the information is gathered, compiled and archived for every member of the group to access. As documents and conversations develop and accumulate, participants may re-visit them, add to them or even discover that their ideas and opinions have shifted over time.

C. Blended Approaches: New Types of Visitors

Ultimately we simply want our visitors to come to our institutions. It is useful to consider how you might invite participants in online programs to come to the museum. While this might not be realistic or possible for all participants, you may find that the online interaction encourages participants to travel to your institution, even if they are located at a far distance.[7] Beyond increasing visitation to the museum, what you may also find is that these learners, having been immersed in an online experience with the museum beforehand, arrive at your institution as a different type of visitor.

Because online learners have spent time interacting with museum staff and thinking about the subject matter, they will arrive prepared to ask different types of questions. They may bring in contextual information that has been studied or may include references to activities and people that were part of the online program. Working with a group of learners who have been immersed in the subject or primed for their museum experience can challenge museum educators to consider new ways of interacting with visitors on-site. It may be useful and necessary to focus more attention on the physical or relational aspects of objects in the collections during these experiences, rather than on other types of "outside information." In developing blended programs, one might also consider whether the online experience occurs before, during or after the in-person visit to the museum.

WHAT DOES THIS MEAN FOR MUSEUMS?

The following are excerpts taken from blog entries written by participating teachers in online workshops over the past two years. These personal, reflective entries provide insights into how online learners are not only experiencing museum-produced content in a new way, but also how their relationship to the museum and their peers has changed over time and place.

I really feel honored to have been able to share my ideas and thoughts with educators from around the country! I am planning to put some lessons into the drop box, and really want to put together a presentation to show on my first day back with my kids! This workshop has definitely helped me with utilizing technology even more, I feel much more confident in venturing out in my teaching approach when it comes to new programs. I am planning on reading through the blogs and wiki areas again as I start to get lesson ideas together for the new school year…

—*Elementary Art Teacher, Niagara Falls, N.Y.*

Because of my work schedule, I have had a hard time attending the live sessions, but today I hope to tune in for a bit before I have to go back to work. I worked on the writing projects and spent a lot more time than I anticipated—it was wonderful! My evenings have been so interesting these past 2 weeks. And making the self portrait over the weekend was fun. I chose to do it in a new way— unlike anything I have ever done before, which was challenging…

—*Primary Grade Teacher, New York, N.Y.*

It took me a while to digest everything that went on in the last several weeks. I thoroughly enjoyed this class and being so "global" was a great experience. The combination of being able to do things at my own pace and convenience, while being able to get together once a week as part of a world force, really, that's what I think it was, has just been the best of both worlds. So often during the live chats I found myself thinking of things just as someone else was saying them or writing them. And then there were the many times that someone said something, or wrote something that blew my mind and made me think in a way I would never had thought of had it been a regular classroom where you submit papers, have them returned, read on your own and don't get the group interaction. As they say, two heads are better than one, and having so many artists and educators in one "room" was fantastic…

—*Elementary Art Educator, Rhode Island*

Over the past four weeks, I have developed a greater understanding of portraits. Seeing both the front and the back of the Van Gogh painting in the galleries was a highlight for me. The photos you took that show how this work is displayed in the museum are fabulous, because it is like being there. I have looked at the virtual tour rooms on the museum's website, but the photos you took were an immediate response to a question posed in the course. Being in Taiwan, it would be impossible to visit the museum and see the work in person, but you made it possible through technology. The possibilities seem endless…

— *Elementary School Teacher, Taipei, Taiwan*

I feel as though I have had the experience of a lifetime to take part in the online workshop then to be asked to present the final PowerPoint at the museum on Friday as a group leader during the on-site program. Although we all met online just two weeks ago, it seems as though I have been conversing, blogging and sharing art viewpoints with you all for years! I am still amazed that we were participating with each other at the same time from all over the world, virtually. I truly appreciate the comments that each of my new friends left for me on the blog. I don't want that part of our class to end.

—*Elementary Teacher, California*

Online learning has the potential to impact museums and museum education practice, not only through expanding our notions of the physical boundaries of our institutions and potential for outreach, but through dramatic shifts in how and when we interact with our visitors. As we interact with these learners from diverse geographic areas, and over longer period of time, we should consider how these exchanges benefit our local participants, our selves and our institutions.

An Online Learner's Perspective

|

Susan Philip Bivona is an Art Educator from Lebanon, New Jersey. She teaches Art, Kindergarten through Fifth Grade, at Mount Prospect School in Basking Ridge, NJ. In 2009, she was voted that National Art Educator of the Year by the National Art Education Association (NAEA). Susan participated in the first online teacher workshop offered at the Metropolitan Museum of Art in the summer of 2007. After that experience, she has continued to enroll in the online programs offered by the Museum. We sent her a series of questions about her online learning experiences and how it has impacted her teaching over the past two years. These are her responses:

Q: Tell us your perspective as an art teacher about participating in an online museum workshop.

Like many people, when I signed up for my first online class, I was both excited and skeptical. Will I be engaged throughout the class? As an art teacher, will this try to replace going to a museum? Will I want to participate or just be a passive listener? Most importantly, will I learn something that I can use in my classroom during this investment of my time?

After taking that first online workshop, all of my questions were answered. I not only participated in the class, but I could not wait to turn on my computer each day. I knew that I had signed up for something special when I received the comprehensive Welcome Packet in the mail two weeks before the start of the class, which included a portrait that I was to "live with" before the start of the workshop. As an art teacher, I am familiar with prints and reproductions and how they can communicate information, but this image we could hold in our hands was also a way for our instructors to reach out to us and say, "Welcome, join us!"

The online workshops that I have taken lasted two weeks, and the participating teachers could log on a week before class to become comfortable in this new learning environment. After the class began, I spent about one hour online each day working on my assignments and projects—some days more and some less. The asynchronous and synchronous elements offered different types of involvement—ways of learning together and on our own.

For me, the synchronous, live sessions were magical. Imagine yourself sitting at your computer in the comfort of your own home, you log on, and see the names of all your classmates, you can chat with each other, talk to each other, use an interactive whiteboard and you can even raise you hand, indicating that you have a question or comment! This setting allowed us the opportunity to interact with the other students and instructors in real time. We took a video tour of the Met, viewed images, PowerPoint presentations and heard guest lecturers.

The interactive features of the whiteboard allowed our instructors to show us a work of art and then, simultaneously, we could respond by typing words describing the artwork right on the whiteboard. Each person in the class could see the information that each participant added to the white board. There were many games and activities to help engage us with the artwork, and all of these experiences could be adapted for our classrooms. The activities also helped us build community with each other as students.

It is also important to state that there was an opportunity for us to create a piece of artwork related to the theme of the online class. We knew this would be a part of the class experience and had individual time to create something meaningful to us. Not everyone was an art teacher in these classes, so students were allowed to work in any medium they felt comfortable with; ranging from art materials such as watercolors or oil paint to quilting to creating a photo collage on Flickr. This gave me a chance to develop a hands-on experience for my elementary students.

One thing that came out of taking my first online course was the realization that a museum is potentially one of the best institutions to offer an online class. The fact that it relies heavily on visual subjects makes it easily accessible and these visual materials give both the instructor and participants the ability to engage quickly. This is important when running a class for a limited amount of time.

Q: What is it like to participate in several online workshops over a period of time? How has your experience of and relationship to the museum evolved?

Like anything, the more you participate, the better you can approach future classes. While the classes integrate technology seamlessly, the first time you take the microphone (to speak in webinar sessions) or make a comment online, there is a bit of awkwardness and preconceived notions. However, pretty quickly you realize it is not much different from a traditional classroom setting. After the first class, you can prepare more thoroughly for discussions and you gain confidence.

Taking an online class complements the museum experience. When you go to a museum, you not only look at the artwork, but you are affected by the location in the gallery, your distance to the artwork and others around you. This can be both good and bad. When you view a work of art online, you get to focus on the individual piece and look at it from a different perspective—one concentrating solely on the work itself.

Viewing art online can cause one to wonder how it really does look in a museum setting, while seeing a painting in a museum can cause one to wish they could analyze it in a different way, up close, perhaps by using technology.

The experience of taking an online workshop has made the museum more accessible to me. Although I have spent quite a bit of time at the Met both as a child and as an adult, I did not use it to its full potential as a teaching resource until I participated in the online workshop. The Metropolitan Museum of Art can be an overwhelming place, to say the least, even to someone comfortable in an art museum. In addition, this workshop has given me access to a contact at the Met and a wealth of online information to which I may never have been exposed without this experience.

When the workshop was over, we were all invited to the museum for an onsite tour. Of course, not all of the participants were able to take advantage of this offer since several lived far away. We were able to tour the museum with our instructor and visit the images we viewed online, giving us a whole new experience with the work of art. Through our time together at the museum, we were able to bond with our classmates and instructors, meet them in person and find out what they were really like. The Metropolitan Museum of Art website is now bookmarked as a favorite and I use it as a resource for my elementary art classes.

Q: You live over 50 miles away from the museum, and in a neighboring state. How do you see value in these types of learning opportunities being at some distance away?

I see almost limitless potential and value though online workshops. The most obvious value focuses on the logistics and content of the classes. As an active board member for the Art Educators of New Jersey, I am fortunate to travel to national conferences and visit many museums as a result. However, at each convention, I meet art teachers who struggle to see perspectives outside their home state. I also know for a fact that as a member of an Executive Board I am one of a small number of educators who have the opportunity to go to a national conference on a regular basis. Through online programs, museums can reach and provide professional development for teachers who may not have opportunities to visit those institutions outside of their state. In addition, the teachers are introduced to a group of educators that can become a part of their own personal learning community.

Online workshops do more than just open a door to a museum or a work of art; they allow the participant to experience the art through a knowledgeable instructor. It allows you to ask questions of the instructor and other classmates in a safe, supportive environment. This is something that should not be underrated.

Also, in an online workshop one could potentially get participants from Minnesota, New Jersey, California, Canada and India—all in the same class! Imagine listening and interacting with people from around the world and hearing their opinions on the subject matter. One of the online museum workshops that I took involved a participant from China and it was fascinating to hear how she might utilize what we learned, from her perspective. How things work in her curricula and classroom shed light on mine.

Q: What kinds of opportunities for community building has this type of online learning experience offered?

After taking just one of the online workshops, I have increased my contact list of professionals in my field. I have also met some professionals outside the field of art education, which is valuable in some ways.

Interestingly enough, I first became aware that the Metropolitan Museum of Art was offering an online workshop through an art education listserv. Even during the first live session, a few of us realized we had met before in Art Ed 2.0, a Ning community (www.ning.com) of Art Educators interested in technology. Art teachers and especially elementary art teachers are often alone in a school, meaning there are no other art teachers in their same building, and no one to bounce an idea off or collaborate. We built community in the online workshop as we worked on our group assignments. Art teachers, like all teachers, are always so very busy at school that there is rarely time to do in-depth research on a topic or an artist. In our online groups, we worked together to research artists and different works of art, and accumulated a tremendous amount of information about the different topics—something that would be almost impossible to do on your own.

Taking an online workshop makes the world just a little smaller and a little flatter, allowing teachers to create and grow their own learning communities where the answers to questions or requests for ideas are just an e-mail or Twitter away. Students in an online class can be from all over the world, giving us the chance to really step out of our community and into a much bigger picture. It has also been interesting to begin to meet classmates at regional and national events, strengthen bonds that started with an e-mail or comment to a classmate's blog post. For example, last summer I met a classmate from the online workshop at the National Art Education Association, Team East Summer Leadership Retreat in New Hampshire. We bonded immediately and created conversation from the common experiences we shared in the class.

This can lead to opportunities for our students to step outside their classroom community to a much broader, worldwide community. For example, through teachers I met in the online workshop, an Artist Trading Card Swap was organized. Artist Trading Cards (ATCs) are miniature works of art, usually done on card stock that are traded between artists. They can be about anything and made with any media, materials, or techniques. My students, along with students from around the world, created their own ATCs; one teacher collected all the cards and then redistributed them to all the teachers who participated. My students received an ATC created by another student, not in our school but from one of the participating schools.

We need to set an example for our students. Learning online will certainly be a part of their futures. My students were fascinated to hear about my experiences with teachers from all over this country and the world. So... what's next? Will the Metropolitan Museum of Art be in my classroom via Elluminate or Skype? Will my students have the chance to build community with museums and students around the world? I think they will, and I cannot wait to see what that will look like.

ENDNOTES

1 For an interesting discussion of the theoretical rationale for place-conscious educa-tion, see "Foundations of Place: A Multidisciplinary Framework for Place-Conscious Education" by David A. Gruenewald. American Educational Research Journal, Fall 2003, Vol. 40, No. 3, pp. 619-654.

2 For an interesting philosophical perspective about the relationships of place and space, see de Certeau, Michel. *The Practice of Everyday Life*, trans. Steven Rendall, University of California Press, Berkeley 1984

3 Place-based education, sometimes called pedagogy of place, has a broad body of literature. For a sampling of museum-related essays, consult *Place-Based Education and the Museum*. Journal of Museum Education, Volume 32, Number 3, Fall 2007, Guest Editors Mark A. Graham and Sharon R. Gray.

4 Dewey, J. *The school and Society* (Rev. ed.). Chicago, IL: The University of Chicago Press.

5 See *Learning From Museums*, chapter 1.

6 For more information about the various strategies and techniques that can be used by educators in synchronous environments, see *Learning in Real Time* by Jonathan Finkelstein.

7 In several of our online teacher workshops, we discovered that several participants from as far away as Florida, California and New Zealand traveled to New York, not only to experience the original works of art, but to share in the culminating experience of the on-site program and to meet their peers and instructors.

CHAPTER 4

The Power of Participation |

Scene: A high school classroom in a Chicago suburb. Students are sitting at their desks, some of them barely awake, some of them asleep. The voice of the Economics teacher drones the following monologue:

> Today we have a similar debate over this. Anyone know what this is? Class? Anyone? Anyone? Anyone seen this before? The Laffer Curve. Anyone know what this says? It says that at this point on the revenue curve, you will get exactly the same amount of revenue as at this point. This is very controversial. Does anyone know what Vice President Bush called this in 1980? Anyone? "Something-d-o-o" economics. "Voodoo" economics.
>
> — From the film *Ferris Bueller's Day Off* (1986)

This memorable scene from the classic John Hughes movie reminds us of the dangers of straying from participatory, learner-centric education. A persistent and even haunting question lingering in the minds of museum professionals is "Are we doing something that is really useful and meaningful for our visitors?" We seek to answer this by using a participatory model of learning that actively seeks input and feedback from the participants. Common to the great diversity of tasks we undertake as museum professionals is the underlying premise that involvement facilitates learning.

Rather than producing programs, exhibitions or projects independent of the end-users or an intended audience, we need to seek out their needs and responses in order to improve the outcome. Gathering information from these constituents, inviting them to contribute and even involving them in planning can help us better understand what success might look like and increase our chances of achieving it. Beyond information gathering, working with these visitors also can help museums become anchored in a community or within a specific group, gaining what is often called "buy in."

As educators, we understand that using a learner-centric and participatory model of teaching means to listen and learn. By inviting others to dialogue, we can better understand needs and perspectives, questions and concerns. As the adage states: "Tell me, I forget. Show me, I remember. Involve me, I understand."[1] We have learned from John Dewey's and other constructivist models of education that it is essential to connect with the learners' experiences in order for the teaching moment to be educative, and to invite individuals to be active agents in their own learning.[2] When we work with teachers to develop a school partnership, use a collaborative approach working directly with students, families or adults and involve visitors and learners, we have the opportunity to craft more meaningful, successful programs and experiences *with them*, rather than merely *for them*.

In our everyday lives, we expect to have control and input in the world around us. We shape and select the media that we consume and make choices about how we spend our time. Instead of responding to an environment that is consistently "top-down," or vertically oriented, we have moved into a realm where a horizontal structure exists. For example, instead of passively receiving information about a movie, we seek out information, make comparisons and even write our own reviews that others can see. Rather than reading the front page of the newspaper, we select articles that we find interesting and mportant, link to them or bookmark them or even add our own news stories and post them online. We are changing from a mentality of consumers to one of producers.[3]

The nature and origin of the Internet itself can be seen as a large-scale network of participation and collaboration. A framework connects people and the ideas that they produce. Increasingly, the Internet not only allows content to be generated by its users, it is primarily driven by them. Files, resources, programming code, software are placed on the Web for others to use, expand upon or take to another level.[4]

The online spaces where interactive learning can occur, and the people who occupy these online spaces, take many forms and are quickly multiplying. Online environments and tools are available for free or at little cost and can be customized and tailored for the specific needs of a group, program or project. These aspects can be extremely appealing to museums as they begin creating learning opportunities with visitors. The participatory nature of the Internet, and the larger culture, can be seen as the proverbial double-edged sword for museums. While we want to invite all visitors into our institutions and encourage dialogue and interpretation, how can museums negotiate the increasing level of participation? How can museums retain their own institutional voice when the voices of visitors are speaking in these new forums accessible by all? Essentially, how can museums remain viable, relevant and authoritative in a participatory world without being authoritarian?[5]

Unfortunately, online environments are not silver bullets for resolving the difficulties of working in a truly participatory and collaborative manner. No digital tool or platform can replace an effective teaching strategy, hard work and direct communication and a respectful, inquiry-based exchange. However, we believe that online collaborative models for learning have not only the potential to alleviate some of the challenges and obstacles that we face in this rewarding yet difficult teaching approach, but in fact have the power to change the way we approach teaching practice. In this chapter we examine a variety of ways that museums can invite visitors to participate in interactive, inquiry-based learning in online environments.

A challenge that online educators face is how to assess whether the learners are actively engaged, since the learners are not physically present. As educators, we know that learning is more than offering an answer to a question. While the tools themselves incorporate a means for participants to provide feedback (emoticons, signals, text chat areas or even live discussion), they do not replace an essential component that must come from the educator: asking participants to provide input and feedback. When working with a group of learners, whether online or in-person, it is important to take the "temperature" of the group, to inquire, to check and to make sure that everyone is onboard. Fortunately, online interaction takes some active forms: participants write blog entries or contribute to a threaded discussion, share files and links, post video and audio or post comments to others' contributions. In short, these digital artifacts exchanged by participants are evidence of interaction. They can provide a measure of the program's success.

The following are several key concepts or cornerstones that describe ways of inviting active, participatory learning in online environments:

A. Sharing Information

When we converse with visitors in the museum, we enter into a dialogic exchange of information about our collections through questions and responses. How does the male ring-tailed lemur grip tree branches as he climbs? What do you notice about the technique used by Mark Rothko in this painting? What types of concerns did Abraham Lincoln express in his written correspondence in 1861?

Both as learners and as instructors, we listen and respond, drawing upon information and personal experiences to make connections and develop ideas and arguments. We recall historical accounts and figures, we remember personal stories or exchanges that illuminate a situation and we use language, writing and gestures to demonstrate our points.

Consider times when you encountered a moment in your teaching or learning when you could not recall a person's name or the date of an event; or the time you needed an illustration, diagram or photograph to communicate your thoughts. Remember the time when a perfect example that would help others understand a concept was on the tip of your tongue but you simply could not recall it.

Learning in an online environment means that we are constantly connected to the largest database of information that the world has seen. Facts, dates, historical records and timelines are at our fingertips and in ever-increasing numbers. In addition to text-based information, we can access photographs, diagrams, illustrations, movies, audio files and multimedia resources that can add immeasurable value to a learning experience. While concern about the quality, scholarship, rigor and reliability of content on the Internet remains an issue, increasingly we find that Internet-based information, especially from accredited institutions such as museums, libraries, universities and archives, is an invaluable educational asset.

Because information is increasingly accessible—and in an online learning encounter it is instantaneous—we find ourselves in a world where we can focus on the how and why of learning. For educators, moving beyond the rote memorization of material in order to think critically about ideas is central to learning. In online learning where the exchange of information can be immediate, more attention can be given to higher-order thinking and to connecting with the personal examples uploaded and shared by the participants. Here are a few examples:

- **Sharing Links:** While this may seem an obvious or simple means of sharing information, the ability to reference information in this way can be a powerful educational tool. Educators and learners alike can post links and use them as launching points for online discussion and interaction. Rather than simply referencing information, participants can actually visit and explore the source itself.

- **Digital Drop Boxes:** When hearing the term "file sharing" one may immediately think of illegal downloads or nefarious Internet trafficking, recalling the legal entanglements of Napster and online music sharing in the mid 1990s. However, when both educators and learners can upload their own examples, documents and presentations, what results is the accumulation of potential ideas and resources that can be utilized by the group. For example, when working with teachers online, participants uploaded their own lesson plans and activity ideas that they had developed themselves so that others could see and use them.

- **Digital Scrapbooking:** Imagine a situation when you have been working with a group on a program or project, perhaps collaborating and brainstorming in order to develop an idea. Notebooks, index cards and papers begin to move across the table. Post-It notes and flip charts become filled with words and diagrams. Examples or models that can be useful are shared and examined. In an online environment, this type of scrapbooking can be a fruitful way of developing a program or project. Because all participants have the power to upload their own ideas directly (which can take the form of links, photos, multimedia files, documents, etc.), the group can quickly assemble a multitude of possibilities to explore.[6]

B. Edit, Refine and Improve: A Collaborative Effort

A central tenet of education is the spirit to improve, develop, expand and deepen. Online learning experiences can provide an ideal moment to invite learners to edit, refine and expand their ideas because online material and information is changeable and adaptable. Participants can type, re-type, delete, copy and paste their own contributions and collaborate with others on a single document. Group collaboration is one of the most powerful facets of online learning, as we find that the "wisdom of crowds" can be exceptionally accurate and offers a multitude of ideas and perspectives. As participants share and collaborate, the final result can be not only more comprehensive than what is typically offered by a single participant, but there is more investment in the final outcome when we invite contributions from the full group.[7]

Perhaps the best example of the power of group collaboration is the wiki, a shared document that can be edited by any number of people. The content is determined by the wiki's creator. Participants can compile information, shift or delete what has been added and even edit another's contribution in a spirit of improving the final outcome. The best known example of a wiki is of course Wikipedia, the collaborative online encyclopedia in which users from across the globe add information, edit refine and expand existing entries. While many have expressed concern that Wikipedia contains information that has not been verified, studies have shown that in fact its articles are overwhelmingly factual and accurate.[8]

C. Roles and Responsibilities: Let Everyone Be an Expert in His Own Way

In online learning environments, all participants access information the same way—at a computer. While the instructor may have access to additional tools and privileges and at times may see information that is not accessible to the learners, all participants are learning and working within the same framework. Often participants in online learning cite its "democratic" nature, allowing everyone to be an equal contributor and stakeholder. Although online learning has its own system of etiquette and group dynamics, participants often mention that they feel confident in asserting their ideas and opinions. They appreciate having more time to consider their contributions before posting them, which is different from live conversation. Perhaps this happens because participants access the experience from home, a familiar and comfortable place, rather than the imposing conditions found in the public space of a museum. Educators can take advantage of this experience by inviting feedback, asking partici- pants to share information about their own areas of expertise or to take on an assigned role that will contribute to the larger group.

Similar to an in-person education program where the educator designates a group leader, it is possible to assign roles in the online learning environment that draw upon the expertise of the individuals. Because the participants have the ability to share information about themselves through e-profiles, e-portfolios or personal blog entries, educators often can determine how participants might lend their expertise in a particular topic. During online teacher workshops that we have conducted, we will often invite participants to serve as "Workgroup Team Leaders" to complete various tasks, given their expertise in a subject area. Or if they are particularly comfortable using technology, they might assist with compiling a document or presentation. In addition to recruiting the talents and expertise of the participants, consider your fellow staff members and how they could contribute to the success of the program. We have found it useful to have an "e-intern" work with the program. This intern of course can be from another city, county or country.[9]

D: Active Reflection

As mentioned earlier, in an online learning experience the interactions and exchanges among participants take some form: blog entries, collaborative wiki documents, presentations that have been created by the group, pre- and post-program online surveys. This process of creating and contributing is an essential aspect of learner-centric, constructivist styles of learning. Technology can capture and archive these process-artifacts so that educators and participants may revisit, re-examine and reflect on their own learning process.

The ability to return to an educational encounter is a profoundly useful tool of online learning. This is rare or impossible in conventional in-person teaching. Not only is it useful for the educator, but participants are able to re-visit threaded conversations, watch webinar recordings, re-read blog entries and download material multiple times. Although online environments vary in terms of their accessibility to the participants, it is possible to make the educational programs and content available for a long period of time, if not indefinitely.

While the educational and evaluative uses are obvious, another useful facet of documenting and archiving is the ability to illustrate and demonstrate an education program for current or prospective donors. In a world of ever-increasing mandates to provide concrete evidence of impact, online learning is uniquely poised to make the learning process tangible and transparent.

By inviting our visitors to become active participants in museum-based online learning experiences, we are building upon the foundations of learner-centric models of museum education that have been growing over the past half-century. Through individual and group involvement, combined with the assets and tools that online learning offers, museums can tap visitors' expertise, curiosity and individualism in ways that are difficult or impossible to achieve in conventional in-person programs.

A Blended Museum-School Collaboration

Photo by David Hayes, Hastings UFSD

BACKGROUND

In the summer of 2008, we were approached by Nate Morgan, an art teacher at the Hillside Elementary School in Hastings-on-Hudson, New York, a few miles north of New York City. He had participated in two online teacher workshops that we offered at The Metropolitan Museum of Art and wondered if we could work together to create an online learning experience with his fourth grade students before and after their in-person museum visit. He also wanted to involve the fourth grade teacher, Jeff Rosof, in the collaboration, along with a graduate student teacher and the technology director at the school.

After an in-person meeting to brainstorm and meet participating faculty and staff, we used several online spaces to brainstorm potential topics and select works of art from the collection. We created a digital scrapbook of ideas, shared links to useful websites and posted images. After some back-and-forth about the topic, we decided to compare a range of portrait paintings from Colonial America to contemporary times. We enlisted the help of other museum staff, as well as an "e-intern" to add further resources to the online environment so that Nate and Jeff could select what to use in the classroom and art studio. We also created an online slideshow of the potential route that students would take during their in-person visit so that the works of art and sequence could be discussed by both the museum staff and the school teachers.

At the start of the program, Nate posted images of the four works of art in an asynchronous online environment called VoiceThread. Students posted their comments and ideas about the portraits, partly to begin a dialogue about aspects that they noticed, but also as a pre-program assessment so that the students could revisit Voicethread again after the program to make additional comments and see what they had learned.

Using synchronous online learning technology, we conducted three live webinar sessions with the fourth grade students over a period of three weeks in October 2008. During these sessions, the students first received an orientation to the online environment and tools, and then took a virtual tour of the Metropolitan. Then they explored the four works of art during the webinars and interacted with the museum staff through text chat, drawing, writing and speaking. They asked questions, responded to one another and explored web features on the Museum's website.

On November 5, the students visited the original works of art that they had been exploring online. During their museum visit, they made connections to the information and concepts that had been introduced during the webinars, and referenced the materials and ideas that had been explored online during the preceding weeks. Understandably, the students were delighted and surprised by many of the physical qualities of the works of art (size, scale, texture, color and gallery location), which were difficult or impossible to experience on the computer.

The following excerpt is from an interview with Nate Morgan and Jeff Rosof on December 16, 2008, during which we reflected on the experience with the students and the process of collaborating online.

Nate, tell us a bit about the reasons why you requested this online/onsite collaboration with the fourth grade students.

Nate: When I took the online teacher workshops in 2007 and 2008, I found it incredibly engaging. The way that we used the technology and exchanged ideas was really interactive. We were able to talk with people all over the world, use the digital whiteboard and speak and chat with each other. This I found to be incredible. It is a great way to stay engaged in the class when you are not the one who is talking. There is a variety of levels and means to stay involved. I also found the online dynamic between the museum educators and the participating teachers was about creating a shared experience, that we were all in this together, working to improve art education for the sake of our students.

So after participating in these online teacher workshops I approached you about maybe doing this at an elementary-school level with students as a way to introduce them to works of art before and after their museum visit.

And Jeff, tell us about how you were approached to be a part of this collaboration.

Jeff: Nate approached me early in the year. He discussed some of the classes he had taken with you and he showed me some of the recordings of the webinars. He showed me some samples and he said, "Look, I have contact with this guy William Crow at the Met, and they are interested in expanding their outreach to schools, possibly by doing a pilot program using online learning with students. What do you think?" Nate and I had collaborated before with other museums and we are often taking students on trips to cultural institutions. I said, "Okay, well, let me think about it," because a classroom teacher's time is always something that you try to guard. I knew that any project takes time, if you want to do it well. So we talked about it some more, and I said, "Okay, well, let's give it a try." The school district where we teach definitely promotes arts in education, so I knew that it would have a good chance of being funded, which Nate helped secure through a grant; but I also knew that it would get administration support, which is important.

Since you both have experience with other types of museum-school collaborations, I am wondering what made this experience different. What did the online interaction allow that has not happened in the past?

Nate: Jeff and I have similar sensibilities in how we work, so I think that we had a lot of common ground from the start. We did have to get a number of people involved from our technology department, and we needed to make sure that we had all of the proper materials and equipment. It became a bigger process then just the two of us. We also had a graduate student teacher involved, and I think that it was an eye-opening experience for her to participate in this type of collaboration.

I think the online collaboration allowed us to achieve a much deeper level of conversation than with typical museum-school programs. Often our experiences in the past have been limited to initial conversations about what you wanted to do or what things you might want to visit. With more traditional programs, there is some conversation about what is happening in the classroom, followed by the museum visit, but then it ends. With this online collaboration, we were able to have conversations before, during and after the museum visit.

Jeff: I definitely think that having in-depth contact with the museum staff made a big difference. It was not just seeing a docent for a one-time visit. You were with us the whole time. And certainly, for the students, you were the star of the program, in many ways. The fact that they were communicating online in real time with a museum educator, they were very impressed by that. Their curiosity was piqued by the technology that this type of thing could even happen. And then when the kids finally met you during the museum visit, it just added even more, not only to their appreciation of the artwork, but also it deepened the personal connection.

Also, having the online space that we could re-visit over time became very useful. I remember the first webinar session with the students, and how Nate and I had high expectations for the students' comments. At first, we were disappointed with the students' comments but then when we went back and heard the recordings, both of us said to each other, "You know what? It was not as bad as we thought." It was nice to be able to hear it again. Very rarely, almost never, can a teacher go back and listen to the teaching that they have done. It is very valuable for teachers to be able to do that. I think you appreciate what your students say more and of course you can learn a little bit more about how you have taught something. I remember that the 10-15 minutes that we spent with the museum staff online, after each webinar, was really useful to debrief about the experience. We talked about what worked and what could have been improved. I really appreciated those moments when we took time to talk. The technology facilitated that aspect.

Nate: Having an online space where all of us could share information and resources was really helpful. And not just between me and Jeff and the museum staff, but also our student teacher was able to participate. We could blog about the experience, share links and the museum uploaded quality images so that we could use them in the classroom. Having this "online commons" for collaboration also enabled us to work on this program outside of normal business hours, away from school.

Jeff: The online environments that we used allowed Nate and I to share projects and approaches in ways that we had not in the past. Nate would ask the students to post comments about a work of art online in the Voicethread, and then we would re-visit those comments in my classroom and keep building on it. So Nate set up some lessons and activities in the art studio, and then we completed them in my classroom. There are a lot of possibilities there for collaboration.

You know, having the online environment to build the collaboration together was helpful in other ways too. Let's say we are having a meeting, and you, as the museum educator, suggest some works of art that we could explore. It is very intimidating for me as a teacher to say, "Ah, I don't really think that's a great one." But if I am home looking at it online, I really can formulate my thoughts and sound somewhat intelligent and say, "You know what? That landscape painting, while priceless, may not work well for my class, for this reason." The online environment affords the time and space to make thoughtful and mportant decisions together.

It is valuable to guard one's time and these types of collaborations can be very time-consuming. How did the online collaboration impact your schedule?

Nate: I am online all the time, so it really did not change the way that I work. I found that I could use small blocks of time with the online format— I could add some thoughts for five or ten minutes between classes or at lunch, and since we were gathering our thoughts and ideas in one place online I could keep re-visiting it. Whether this way of working is a good or bad thing is for others to decide. But personally, I like being able to work on projects this way.

Jeff: For myself, I really did not have time during the day to go online. So I did a lot of it from home, which obviously would be impossible without the technology. Once I started blogging and adding to the site we created I actually enjoyed it because it was just a way to journal my thoughts. It was nice to have them recorded.

Tell us more about how the technology facilitated the students' interaction with the museum.

Jeff: Anything with technology, at this point, is very exciting to the children. Something that is new is very exciting. So they were very thrilled to be the only class doing this, the first class to be doing this, the fact that it was a pilot program. Now, ten years in the future, that will just be commonplace, but for the moment the technology piece added real excitement. The students' ease and comfort level with the technology was still developing over the course of the program. The webinars also excited them. Having the whole class together online was different from calling on students in class. They said, "Wow, I actually got to speak into this microphone and all of my classmates heard it." Now of course everyone hears one another when they speak in our typical classroom, but this was different. It added a different layer of importance to their comments and ideas and of course, the fact that the museum educator was in New York City, hearing them and responding to them, was a thrill for them, something unique. They had their little piece of that pie, of that power.

Nate: Whenever teaching becomes a monologue—with the teacher calling out questions and the students responding one at a time, there is a danger that there is much less engagement. The online experience involved them through speaking, writing, drawing and chatting.

Jeff: I think that sometimes classroom instruction can be seen as one-dimensional. The teacher is speaking, a student can raise his hand and speak, everyone is supposed to be in a listening position and everyone is supposed to have their eyes on the speaker. This technology helped to make learning three-dimensional. There is more than one thing going on at once and suddenly it is okay for a student to not necessarily be completely, 100% focused on the speaker. Students can use the chat area, and with some direction, their comments stay focused and on topic, while they are seeing an image. Then ten seconds later, one of their classmates is sharing some information because they have the microphone. This can happen in a typical classroom in different ways, but the online learning environment allows students to share and contribute in many ways, and all at the same time.

Do you think this type of multi-tasking or multi-layered interaction is positive for student learning?

Jeff: I think that it probably mirrors very much what happens in their lives outside of school. When they are at home, there might be a TV or an iPod on, they might be working on the computer, IM-ing a friend and doing something else. Fourth graders are probably just starting to do some of those things. But certainly by middle school they are communicating and interacting this way.

What kind of impact did the online learning have on the students' experience at the museum?

Jeff: I remember when we were in the Modern Art galleries, and saw the portrait by Chuck Close. Just to see the size and the detail, that just was impossible to understand on a 19-inch computer screen. Even when I put it up on the 72-inch SMARTboard, it is still not the size of the canvas, which is enormous. And secondly, you lose detail that was really important. Now, I know that this project, theoretically, can go out to people in California who will never be able to get to the Met, and that is just a reality. But of course it is always important for the students to understand the power of the original objects in the museum and to experience them.

Besides getting to travel to the museum and see the original objects, they really enjoyed the contact with a real person via the technology. That was a highlight for them. They could not wait to meet you, it was almost like you were a celebrity to them. Even when I told them that I was not going be in school today because I am coming down to the Met, they said, "Say hi."

The technology and the interaction made them curious and got them in the door, so to speak. But in the end, I think you prepared very informative and interesting programs. We cannot overlook the fact that there needs to be people who know how to interact with the kids and know the subject matter.

Nate: I think that the students had more investment in their experience at the museum because of the online learning that happened beforehand. Their response to you during their visit was not something that I normally see on a typical museum trip. Students tend to be very aware that they are there for one day, for the one hour, for the one presentation. They also see the museum visit as a presentation. Because of our collaboration, they really responded to you, as if you were our teacher. And that is a different way of interacting with the museum.

Jeff: I was really impressed during the museum visit with the connections that the students made between the online sessions and the in-person experience. But besides retaining the information from those sessions, I think that it was important for the children to understand that technology isn't everything. I remember when they stood in front of the original painting and said "Wow. I didn't see that on the computer."

So now that the collaboration has finished, will it have any impact on your teaching in the future?

Jeff: We focus on Colonial America in the spring, and it will be interesting to see what kinds of connections the students make to the colonial works of art that we examined in this program. We can use the online materials again and even watch the webinar recordings to re-visit the works of art in the museum.

Also, tying it back to student learning, a key idea is connecting reading and writing to all learning experiences. It is not enough now to just solve a problem. Tell us how you solved this problem. Students do a science experiment and then they write about how they solved the problem. This is a big push in K-12 education and I try to incorporate this into the classroom. I could see how the digital environments would be great to capture student learning in this way.

So much classroom education is top-down, even if we do not want it be. In the end, the teacher is still presenting the information. A lot of times there is a right and a wrong. It is important to try new things, to have a more open-ended approach. As far as the technology, I do not want to start next year without having some type of program on my plate to keep trying new things. With the help of our technology director, I would like to find ways of connecting with other cultural institutions.

Nate: Well, one thing that I am always impressed with, especially since I see the students once every six days and have such limited time with them, is what they remember from two years before, or last year, or even a month ago. It will be interesting to see what happens in the spring when Jeff starts his unit on Colonial America. I hope that when the students start studying that time period they recall the colonial portraits that we explored in this collaboration. One of the most exciting aspects of using the technology is being able to re-visit these projects with the students over time. This aspect is really appealing to me, since I have such limited time with each class.

What would you tell other schools that were considering this type of online collaboration with a museum?

Nate: I think, as with anything that a teacher does in her classroom, that a program like this does not work if it is just you doing all the work. It really has to be back and forth between what you do and what your collaborators do and what the students do.

Jeff: Working with teachers can be very difficult. Teachers are a group of people that are used to being in control of their environment. Many teachers do not like giving up the control or admitting that they are not the experts. In this online collaboration, the technology enabled everyone to be an expert in his or her own right. I would never be able to present a work of art the way you can. You would not be able to work with the children in the classroom format that we do. This type of format lets everyone bring his own interests, knowledge and skills to the table.

ENDNOTES

1 This teaching adage, often cited among schools and teachers, is attributed to Confucius, c. 450 B.C.E.

2 John Dewey, *Experience and Education*

3 Thomas L. Friedman, *The World is Flat*

4 For more information about an organization that aims to bring together individuals who want to share their creative work without the burdens of traditional copyright, see www.creativecommons.org.

5 See M. MacArthur, *Can Museums Allow Online Users to Become Participants?* in *The Digital Museum* for more discussion.

6 A useful tool for digital scrapbooking is Google Notebook, www.google.com

7 For an interesting exploration of the power of groups, see James Surowiecki's *The Wisdom of Crowds.*

8 Giles, Jim. Special Report: *Internet encyclopedias go head to head, Nature* 438, 900-901 (15 December 2005) Published online 14 December 2005

9 We have been fortunate to work with several "e-interns" both from area universities and abroad, including Chelsea Kelly from Vassar College (NY) and Mercedes Colombo, an educator from Buenos Aires, Argentina.

CHAPTER 5

Museums and Online Communities of Learners |

> The community stagnates without the impulse of the individual. The impulse dies away without the sympathy of the community.
> — *William James*

> A community is like a ship—everyone ought to be prepared to take the helm.
> — *Henrik Ibsen*

M any museums that were founded in the mid-19th century were intended by their proponents to be loci and catalysts for community building. Institutions such as the Metropolitan Museum of Art, the American Museum of Natural History, The Boston Museum of Fine Arts and the Art Institute of Chicago were founded on the educational premise that visitors, many from immigrant communities, would be welcomed into these halls of learning and that museums could act as a civilizing force. As these new citizens came into the United States in large numbers, museums were opened, in part, to invite these new neighbors to share a common language, strengthen common values and build a shared history.[1]

Reflecting on these ideas today, we might be critical of notions of assimilation or attempts to "civilize" others, but the idea that museums could be centers of learning and enjoyment for different communities still holds value today. As author and museum management expert Harold

Skramstad noted, "Museums, like other community institutions such as colleges and universities, theaters and opera houses, were often built and in business before roads were named or paved. They functioned to anchor and stretch the communities for which they were created."[2] Museums act as beacons and catalysts for communities. In the 20th century, many museums proclaimed themselves "community-based" according to their founding principles. They sought members of their immediate communities to explore their collections and strived to be active agents while developing exhibitions and programs. The act of engaging the community is not only a laudable notion but a necessity: to remain viable, museums now must acknowledge and involve communities. Community leaders are invited to become museum board members and community audience development initiatives are ubiquitous.

Digital technologies have facilitated new ways for communities to assemble and interact with organizations to an extent that was impossible even a decade ago. Not only can members of these communities create and share ideas and resources instantaneously and easily, but they are no longer limited by geography. Prior to telecommunications and the Internet, communities were usually limited by their physical neighborhoods, work environments and local in-person contact. We increasingly see that community is no longer bound by place. In fact it has been noted that traditional geographically-based communities often require members to adhere to a set of norms rooted in face-to-face experience, at times requiring them to suppress their individualism and uniqueness.[3]

Today online communities develop around topics that range from model cars to recipe swapping to political activism. Members of these communities may live close to each other and occasionally meet, while others will never have a face-to-face encounter with their peers. Online communities may be connected to organizations and institutions and even make recommendations to the leadership of these entities through online interactions, forming what has been termed "radical trust."[4]

This chapter will examine how museums can harness the power of community through online interaction, not only as a means of outreach to current and potential visitors but also to facilitate rich and meaningful learning experiences that build upon the constructivist, learner-centric approaches currently found in museum education practice. Museums can offer expansive opportunities to learn in community—a means to access knowledge that is within, among and between us.[5]

WHO ARE THESE ONLINE COMMUNITIES AND HOW DO THEY WORK?

Although the importance of communities within the museums' walls has become clear, the presence of online communities that virtually enter and encircle the museum can be more difficult to decipher. While museums are increasingly equipped to measure visitors to their websites, there is a rising wave of online visitors who use museum-produced online materials to create their own websites, materials or interactions with others.[6] Social networking tools such as MySpace and Facebook have now been tapped to create museum-produced "groups" that connect with the institution and greatly facilitate the flow of information about upcoming events, much to the delight of museum marketing staff. These social networking tools are expanding and increasing in profound ways. They are clearly useful, and we see in them great opportunities for museums to facilitate qualitative learning experiences for specific groups of visitors.

FROM GROUP TO COMMUNITY

Earlier in this book, we described how group online interaction and participation among individuals could unleash incredible power. However, not all groups are functioning as communities; although participation may be high, community has not been formed. As we know in our own "analog" lives, individuals are brought together by external circumstances and sometimes do not function effectively as groups. Effective group function requires a delicate balance. To move toward its goal, a group will often alternate between completing tasks and negotiating relationships among members and their tasks. Frequently groups pass through several stages (sometimes described as forming, storming, norming, performing, transforming) before they arrive at a point where they can function most effectively.[7]

Researchers in online pedagogy often discuss how online communities are different from online groups and how they require more than participation. They must include common elements if they are to progress successfully oward an educational goal. These elements include the ability to build mutual trust, a sense of belonging and membership and a sense that the community is sharing in the educational process.[8] While some of these qualities can emerge from high-functioning online groups, an effective online community is often fostered by an educator or teaching presence who creates a climate of mutual respect and sharing.

The following examples illustrate elements that can contribute to successful online learning in communities and how the interactive qualities of the Web provide unique assets to this type of educational encounter.

A. Uploading a Personal Culture

In third-grade classrooms across the United States, one might hear the phrase "community begins with me" as students begin to learn about the world that surrounds them. By first seeing and examining themselves as integral parts of the community, students are better able to understand how relationship and cooperation among others is at the core of community.

This phenomenon of starting with the individual user often takes the form of building a user online profile. This can take many forms: an E-Profile, E-Portfolio, a list of interests or simply contact information and location. A decade ago there were concerns about the amount of information that individuals place online. Now there are ways to make careful, considered choices about what is visible online, and with whom information is shared.

Fig. 1: Example of an e-Portfolio in the Epsilen Global Learning System

Creating a personalized space online, or establishing one's online social presence, is an important step in building an online community.[9] In the museum field, we often encourage visitors to "take ownership" of the museum. We open our doors to welcome them. We offer comfortable cafes to sit and have coffee, ways of customizing their experience and creating opportunities for membership. While it might initially appear this "space marking" is self-centered, the idea is to encourage users to communicate information and share it with a larger group. As individuals personalize, customize and expand their social presence online, they establish a stronger online identity, thus providing more possibility of connection to a larger community.

As we see in Fig. 1, the user is adding photos, background information, interests and ideas. Essentially the user is creating a personal culture by using these artifacts in a localized, personalized space. This process is an important one, as individuals are able to carve out a space that is unique to them, rather than assuming one that has been dictated by organizations and institutions.[10]

B. Informal Learning in Online Museum Communities

Different from organized, curriculum-based institutions such as schools, museums often subscribe to theories of informal learning. Rather than being motivated by external factors (grades and other formalized learning tructures), museums aspire to create educational experiences that tap into the learner's own curiosity and interest. In informal learning, a specific pedagogy may not be rigidly in place, and learners become self-directed and often act in ways that are more spontaneous.

Informal learning in online communities may include the active presence of the museum, but these communities frequently take on a life of their own. While the online community is connected to the institution and is aligned with its mission, it may also push into other terrain that serves the community's membership. Online chat or banter may connect with other topics, perhaps not related to the educational content at hand, but as a means to keep members engaged. Of course, this type of informal learning and exchange happens frequently in-person in museums, as visitors socialize, meet in the café to have a coffee or use the museum as a launching point into other activities.

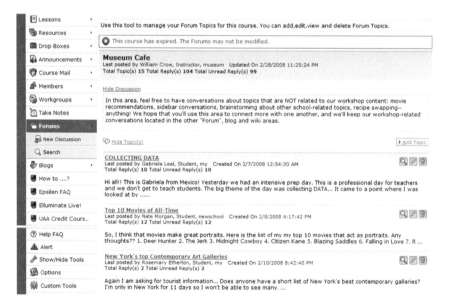

Fig. 2: Example of Museum Café in the Epsilen Global Learning System

In the following example, teachers participating in an online workshop are also invited to interact in the Museum Café, a threaded discussion area where they may exchange information and interact on topics not necessarily connected to the content of the workshop.

C. We're All in This Together

A museum educator is surrounded by a noticeably excited group of 25 fifth-grade students who just arrived at the natural history museum. After she welcomes the group, she takes a quick poll to see how many students have visited the museum before. A girl describes how she came several years ago to see the dinosaur bones with her father. Another student mentions that he has never visited this museum, but that his mother teaches paleontology at a local university and they visited other science museums where they used to live. After a brief discussion, the rules of the museum are reviewed and the group enters the first gallery, filled with fossils from thousands of years ago.

The museum educator invites the students to examine one in particular, walk around it, examine it closely and think of a word that comes to mind that would describe it. "Scaly," says one student. "Like an old rock," says another. "It reminds me of a shell that I saw on the beach once," adds another. Another student interjects, "Oh yeah, I've seen those before. But this one is much bigger." The conversation continues, and the educator inserts key pieces of information and questions from time to time to direct, explain and focus the students' observations. The group continues building and expanding upon one another's ideas.

This type of educational encounter can be seen in museums that subscribe to learner-centric, inquiry-based models of teaching. Learners are invited to observe, describe, make connections and comparisons, build inferences and draw conclusions based on evidence. As they interact, there are opportunities for the learners to learn from each other in addition to their instructor.

In an online community, there are a multitude of opportunities for participants to learn and have peer-to-peer interaction. These may include comments to blogs, threaded discussion and chat or e-mail exchanges among members. They may visit others' E-Profiles or E-Portfolios to make connections between participants' contributions and his/her location, background or interests.

Some online communities, including those that we have facilitated through the museum, are closed communities, meaning that they are open only to those participants who have enrolled and who are actively seeking this type of learning experience. Within this shared online space, and as shared experience builds, the community begins to form bonds of trust that allow for deeply meaningful interaction. Just as when an unexpected observer enters an in-person learning situation, or when online "guests" enter an online community of learners, there is a danger of disrupting the trust and rapport that has been established.

Online communities may become internally driven by members who keep the community actively exchanging information and ideas. Thus

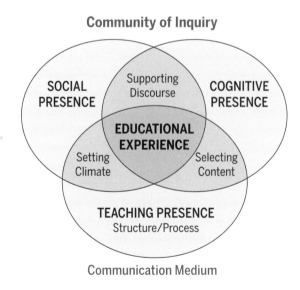

The Community of Inquiry model. Copyright 2007 R. Garrison, T. Anderson, W. Archer and L. Rourke et al., University of Calgary. Reprinted with permission.

the role and the educational approach taken by the museum may be closer to that of a facilitator or moderator of peer interaction. While it is important that the educator maintain a teaching presence during the interaction, she may guide conversation, offer possible resources and information, invite the group to consider relationships between ideas and pose inquiry-based questions. This type of teaching presence, currently practiced in many museum education programs, is also possible in an online community of learners.

THE COMMUNITY OF INQUIRY MODEL

While we all understand how knowledge can be constructed with individuals, we often find that learning is best achieved when tied to a social act. The nature of constructing knowledge is social and museums contribute to the creation of experiences that connect to the visitors' own lives. Learning in community often means negotiating meaning and contributing to a pluralism of voices and ideas. Museums are places where people can meet, make friendships with others who share similar interests or where they can be a part of something larger than themselves. Because museums increasingly value dialogue not only about the collection but also about how it connects with communities and larger ideas, online learning creates a space where this dialogue can occur.

In recent years, the learning power of online communities has come into focus as a fertile area for research and investigation. As online communities work together in a spirit of sharing and curiosity facilitated by knowledgeable and skilled educators, these communities have the power to create a climate where knowledge can be constructed and examined with a high degree of proficiency. The Community of Inquiry (COI) model developed by Garrison, Anderson and Archer in the mid-1990s proposed a conceptual order for the various elements of presence necessary for effective learning in community: social, teaching and cognitive. A tool for the use of computer-mediated communication in supporting an educational experience, the COI model constructs knowledge through the intersection of these elements.

As we see, the educational experience occurs most effectively within the intersection of the important elements of social, teaching and cognitive presence. Informal and inquiry-based models of learning, such as those offered by museums, combined with the powerful assets of online learning environments and teaching strategies, create educational experiences that parallel and inform those we currently value in our institutions.

COMMUNITY MOTIVATION AND EXPANSION

When members of online communities are working together toward a common purpose, we find that the members are motivated to learn from each other and often seek out additional shared experiences. While they may still be engaged in individual or small group activities, the cohesion and sense of community that builds over time can encourage the community to create new activities related to their educational encounter. In the example of Susan Bivona's case study (Chapter 3), we saw how the members of the online teacher workshop organized an exchange of Artist Trading Cards (ATCs) on their own, sparked by the content of the workshop itself and facilitated by the online medium.

Another powerful example from our blended teacher workshops is how members of the learning community consistently want to attend the in-person component of the program at the museum, not only to experience the original objects *but to do so with the other members of the workshop*. While they express both intrinsic and extrinsic forms of motivation for joining the group in this way, they most often discuss how they desire to be part of a shared experience that builds upon the online experience.

We have also seen that online participants, just as participants in onsite programs, share their positive experiences with others and encourage peers to participate in future programs. This creates a different type of community—one not bound by computer cables, hardwired or wireless connections—but a community of learners who share a common experience. Online participants have mentioned that professional isolation was a motivation to enroll in the program. Through sharing their experiences with others and encouraging their peers to join them online, we find that new "in-person" communities and relationships are forged.

Online Learning as a Way to Access and Involve New Communities

Museums constantly seek to expand their constituencies by connecting with existing communities. Museum staff network with community leaders, exchange mailing lists and invite key groups in the hopes of welcoming more visitors. Online learning has great potential for both connecting with existing communities and forging new ones. But beyond outreach, online learning can forge communities that museums may not have previously considered—both among their visitors and among the museum's staff. This case study presents two perspectives about how community online learning can not only enhance a museum's outreach to underserved visitors and other organizations, but also how it can transform the museum structure itself.

David Gordon is the executive director of the Living Through Learning Foundation, whose mission is to keep all children with chronic health conditions in the U.S. connected to learning opportunities and peers through the use of technology. Previously, David worked with children with cancer and blood disorders as an education liaison for the LEARN program at the Tomorrows Children's Institute at Hackensack, New Jersey, University Medical Center. In the following narrative, he describes the situation of Charise, a sixth-grader who is battling a chronic health condition,

and how Charise and her family find new ways to connect with a museum and each other as a result of online learning.

Approximately 15 percent of students in the United States are diagnosed with chronic health conditions and roughly half of these youths report that their chronic health condition hampers their daily activities (Perrin 2007). In addition, more than two million school-aged children a year in the U.S. will be hospitalized for a chronic health condition. For children with more severe health conditions, it is not unusual to miss weeks, months or even entire school years, causing social and academic isolation. Often these students are not seen as learners at all; just "sick kids" whose education can wait while they receive treatment. Most children want and need to stay connected, not only for the sake of some normalcy in their lives, but also as a means to improve their outlook and state of mind.

Charise just finished 5th grade. She was diagnosed with leukemia three years earlier and so she has had a difficult time medically and also with school. Because she would often miss classes to receive medical care, she often expressed feeling "out of the loop" and said that she didn't have many friends or was often confused about what was going on in class.

Sixth grade proved to be different. She was finally having a good experience, making lots of friends, and science (her most difficult subject) was her favorite class. Just before the school year ended, it was discovered that her leukemia had relapsed. This meant even more intensive treatment than the first time, including the serious procedure of having a bone marrow transplant, which would include over 100 days of isolation. During this time, Charise would not be allowed to leave her house or the hospital. Charise was very sad that she was missing school and would be out of the loop once again. But what if she never had to be out of the loop?

Working with Charise, her school and her family, I learned more about her interests and the curriculum that the sixth grade class was exploring. With the assistance of an area educational technology consortium and the expertise of the staff at the New York Hall of Science, a series of live, synchronous webinars were developed and scheduled so that Charise could continue to learn. She participated in a series of science activities throughout the summer, both from home and from the hospital. These online webinars between Charise and the museum staff included dissections, cell anatomy, and viewing micro organisms through a microscope—all in real time. Moreover, she participated in virtual floor exhibit tours with the science center staff. She had virtual tours that involved light, sound, physics and many more topics. Online learning makes it possible for any child with a chronic health condition to access virtual field trips, their school classroom or even to contact family members outside of the U.S. who, for a variety of reasons, may not be able to visit in person. Even though she was out of school, her love for science didn't have to suffer. For Charise, every Thursday at 2 pm, regardless of her medical situation or temporary isolation, was science class.

Online learning of course is not without its challenges. In our experience we have had to overcome a number of problems. Specifically, varying modem speeds which negatively affected the audio and video feeds, inaccuracies and miscommunications regarding time and date due to various time zones, and the difficulties with creating a mobile floor unit to allow the home learner a more meaningful virtual experience. With this format a learner, school and museum need nothing more than a computer, web camera, internet access and a cart.

In conversations with both Charise and her family these online learning experiences had a profound impact on them in positive and unanticipated ways. One such conversation took place after a live webinar with the science center on the topic of light. Both parents reported that for the rest of the afternoon and into the evening the family as a whole discussed light: prisms, sunlight, the color spectrum and other related topics Charise had learned about that day. As Charise's mother said to me: "Her virtual field trip turned into an experience for the whole family. We could all discuss and learn more about this interesting topic, which in no way connected to Charise's illness."

Children with chronic health conditions benefit from online learning experiences in many ways. These experiences allow learners to "leave" their room and experience a part of the world through their mind. It allows these students to stay active in the learning process even when they are feeling isolated. In addition, when their ability to have a set routine is diminished, they can choose to participate in a series of learning-based activities, just as Charise did, to gain a level of control and routine in an otherwise uncertain future. For the families of learners with chronic health conditions, the impact may be unexpected and quite striking. The impact that a chronic health condition has on family dynamics is well documented. However, online learning can provide purposeful activities in which the whole family can participate, offering a true paradigm shift in this field of study.

These types of connections should not end with the individual student who has a chronic health condition. In fact, recently at one hospital in New Jersey multiple families were connected to the same cultural institution simultaneously. In this case, one child was at home, the other at the hospital and both connected to the same science center for a "floor tour" of exhibits. These types of multiple connection points, while currently unique, should become commonplace in the near future. During the experience described above, the Chief of Pediatric Oncology discussed these types of opportunities not just as novel but necessary for the well-being of the learners.

In my current work as executive director of the Living Through Learning Foundation, our goal is to provide an online community for treating institutions, cultural centers, children with chronic and serious illness and their families. Our target population of learners who are typically isolated can now stay connected to their community and classmates and also meet new "virtual classmates" through online learning experiences. Communities of children with chronic health conditions can connect, learn and even teach one another. Online interaction provides these children and their families a means to regain control over an essential life function—learning.

The second case study is from Chris Lawrence, Senior Manager of Digital Learning, from The New York Hall of Science. Recently, The Hall created a Digital Learning department. In the following case study, he shares with us their experience on how to use new technologies to foster different communities of learners, and how the Digital Learning department functions in The Hall museum structure.

There is a perception that digital interactions and modalities are less valid than "real" experiences. This real/un-real dichotomy is not only false, it is out of step with how the 21st century operates. Increasingly the definition of what is real and what is technologically enhanced or enabled is blurred. Business easily integrates communication and networking concepts into their evolving tool kit. Collaboration in the workforce is often facilitated by information technology. Marriages, familial relationships, entertainment and the acquisition of social capital are all supported by the technological advancement of the last 20 years. In Robert D. Putnam's revelatory book, *Bowling Alone*, he discusses the Internet as having the potential to aid the decline of community in America or be a powerful mechanism to change the dire trends. In Putnam's final chapter, he issues societal challenges for technology when he says, "Let us foster new forms of electronic entertainment and communication that reinforce community engagement rather than forestalling it." Perhaps even more prophetically he offers routes he saw where the Web could strengthen social capital. What he prescribed—citizen journalists, content creators rather than receivers, connected micro-communities around niche interests that strengthen face-to-face interactions—are all aspects of "Web 2.0," the buzzword given to the web software functions that make up the Social Web. Today, perhaps the answer to bowling alone is networked Wii Bowling.

Against this ever shimmering backdrop, educating and activating learners for the 21st century can be a dizzying task. The speed and sophistication of communications technology, the digital infrastructure and a global economy create a complex learning landscape and one that only promises to diversify. The next generation of learners, workers and leaders will need to be sophisticated, knowledgeable, enthusiastic and empowered. During the summer of 2007, The New York Hall of Science moved towards trying to address and plan for the young century's emerging learners by creating the Digital Learning department. Previously, The Hall had been implementing programs that used educational technology. This momentum was exemplified by initiatives like the National Science Foundation-funded Crime Scene Information Technology (CSIT) Forensic Science curricula and the Virtual Visit videoconferencing program. With the launch of the Digital Learning department, The Hall created a dedicated team that could manage these programs, design ways to utilize other technologies and research trends in both the field and society.

At The Hall, digital technology recasts our concept of communities, creating a true plurality that encompasses everything from narrowcasting to global interactions. In the Digital Learning department, we have attempted to embrace this approach by cultivating a broad spectrum of communities based on programming needs and outreach. When we design new programs that employ online learning tools, our goal is to use them in ways that lay the groundwork for people talking and learning about science by creating a communal space for science learning. The transformative nature of the technology is that it makes us closer. We can connect to an 11-year-old cancer patient once a week while she is home-bound and talk about cells, optical illusions and dry ice, all while giving her a window to socially interact from her bedroom. We become a valuable player in her family's recovery road, and a small community as mentioned in the first case study. We can run online courses for teachers struggling to change their teaching practice to an open-ended inquiry approach, giving them space for reflection and a community to support each other's work. After a week of threaded discussions about what third graders could not handle during a hands-on science exploration, one brave teacher tried it. She also documented it and when she posted her photos along with a written recap of the successful day, the conversations changed. Instead of trepidation about the labs we were asking them to try, the teachers were inspired by their colleague and soon we had not only photos of many third graders getting dirty with science, but videos and the participating teachers were emboldened to begin adapting the lesson plans, posting their own and making honest reassessments of their own techniques. By tackling small projects and taking the time to strengthen the human element of these digital experiences, we feel confident we are growing our institutional definition of community.

One surprise to me is the establishment of an unexpected learning community—The New York Hall of Science employees and thus the institution itself. What we have found with much of the tools, software and activities that we use in our education programs is that they are useful and applicable to many at The Hall. Almost immediately, the education department at large was an eager audience for what we were doing within Digital Learning. The staff who manage and teach our after-school and weekend science programs and enrichment camps began incorporating blogging as a reflective practice for the participants as well as the instructors. They built podcasting, digital photography and social networking into their curriculum. The education department began using an internal wiki for documentation, storage, communication and as a collaborative project space with colleagues outside the Hall.

One initiative that began as an experiment in our small department but now permeates throughout The Hall has been our foray into social networking via the online service, Ning. Ning allows users to build their own social networks and control the rules that govern how they are used, managed and joined. The networks allow for blogging, chat, forums, groups, photos, video, audio and additional interactive features. First we used this dynamic tool as a broadcast platform for the podcasting after-school science program, but quickly others were building networks for projects like collaborating with science centers in India, communicating with teachers in year-long professional development programs, and for an online forum for a cohort of science center professionals who work with youth staff. However, I would like to highlight three Ning networks that illustrate how this technology-learning tool impacted the institution on a larger scale.

The Hall employs over 80 "Explainers." Explainers are high school and college students who work our exhibit floor interacting with our visitors, engaging them about the science exhibited and facilitating their learning experience at The Hall. They are paid an hourly wage and there is system in which they can advance and even in some cases become full-time staff. No one exemplifies what we call the "Science Career Ladder" better than our Senior Vice President of Education and Public Programs, Preeti Gupta. She began her executive journey from Explainer to Vice President as a Queens' teenager! Sustaining communications with the large corps of current Explainers and the hundreds of alumni Explainers has always been an issue for the Hall. Creating a Ning network seemed like a plausible solution to this challenge. The site "Clumpology" was created and it became an instant sensation. The management team quickly had an eager community where they began to disseminate information, create groups around projects, provide reflective space for the Explainer's work experiences, as well as keeping those who moved on connected. Today "Clumpology" has over 280 members, 16 groups of interest and 74 videos.

The second Ning network is our "My Sci" project. It was designed as an outreach to both the youth and parents involved in all the various out-of-school-time learning opportunities we offer. The Ning platform and its high level of customization by the user make it an excellent tool for a variety of purposes and audiences. We wanted to connect with parents to market our programs, highlight their children's work and cultivate a community that viewed The Hall as a valuable learning resource. We also wanted to establish "club houses" for the participants, a space where we could have them comment on the programs, answer questions, contemplate science concepts, post their work in multimedia formats and socialize with each other both while at the Hall and later at home. "My Sci" now has over 230 community members, six clubhouses and over 100 blog posts and comments from participating students.

The third and final example of how The Hall uses social networks to build community and foster online learning represents a move from being a tool used within the education department to one that the institution as a whole utilizes. A network has been created for all The Hall employees and trustees. The goal is to foster a space where staff could discuss, share and dream ways forward for The Hall. Initially it was launched as a way to follow a team of senior executives on a trip to Bay Area science centers. We followed their conversations, watched videos and posted questions we would like to ask our counterparts they were meeting. This activity sparked productive, focused brainstorming and reflection while building a better understanding of one another as co-workers. Through nurturing these many purposed networks, we learn more about ourselves and become inclusive to the many voices and ideas in the learning process.

I am biased, but The Hall is a fantastic place with iconic architecture, hands-on exhibits that make science tangible, and diverse programming. But what we pride ourselves on is that we are a people-based institution. We believe that without conversations around our exhibits and spaces that facilitate interaction and communication, we would underserve our audience and mission. Our move into digital representations of ourselves must keep this core value as we attempt to integrate the speed of technology into our practice. In the Digital Learning department, we adhere closely to this philosophy. I take Putnam's challenge personally when he implored those working in this new media information age to use these powerful tools to buck the trends that he ominously charted in *Bowling Alone*. None of the projects and the resulting communities I have described are very large, but in aggregate they represent the expansion of "what we do" into many more homes, classrooms and learners' lives. Along the long tail of all this work, we hope to nurture communities of many interests not only with us but also with each other. Are these not "real" interactions we are providing and facilitating for our publics? The technology is not the medium. People are still the medium in our programs. The technology is simply the vessel.

While managing this experiment of having a Digital Learning think-tank at The Hall, the lesson for me as a museum professional is how important it is to have people who are both immersed in learning and in the application of these new technologies. We pride ourselves as being a kind of hybrid between the IT and education professional, able to speak both languages while charting a holistic forward course. It is my belief that learning of all kinds needs to embrace this multi-disciplinary approach and that the thoughtful use of technology will be a powerful constructivist toolkit that no institution with an educational mission can ignore. With the support of The Hall the Digital Learning staff is excited and energized to help define 21st-century skills and tools. With the use of online learning and digital learning our intention is to include and spark many communities along that envisioned trajectory, whether they are half a world away, in the same zip code or down the hallway.

ENDNOTES

1 See *Riches, Rivals and Radicals: 100 Years of Museums in America* by Marjorie Schwarzer, AAM, 2006.

2 See *An Agenda for Museums in the 21ˢᵗ Century* by Harold Skramstad. Daedalus, Summer 1999.

3 Shaffer, C. and Anundsen, K. *Creating Community Anywhere*. Los Angeles: Tarcher/ Perigee Books, 1993.

4 See www.radicaltrust.ca/ for more information about how influence, rather than control, guides commerce, institutions and communities.

5 See David Weinberger, *Everything is Miscellaneous*.

6 See Slate Audio podcast tours, for example, www.slate.com

7 See Smith, M. K. (2005) 'Bruce W. Tuckman - forming, storming, norming and performing in groups, the encyclopaedia of informal education, www.infed.org/thinkers/ tuckman.htm.

8 See Shea, P., Swan, K., and Pickett, A. "Teaching Presence and Establishment of Community in Online Learning Environments." Sloan Consortium, 2004.

9 See Pratt, K. "The Electronic Personality." Unpublished doctoral dissertation, Human and Organizational Systems Program, Fielding Graduate University, 1996. Referenced in Palloff and Pratt, *Building Online Learning Communities*, 2nd ed, 2007.

10 See Thomas L. Friedman, *The World is Flat*, p. 476.

Conclusion |

s the Internet expands and diversifies, connection, communication and collaboration have dramatically increased. We are
changing not only the ways that we share information and
ideas, but also how we see ourselves and the world around us.
Museums, already deeply engaged in how people make meaning
of the world around them, are becoming more equipped to take an
expanded role in how people interact and learn from the museum's
collections, its staff and with one another. Museums must now see these
new communication methods not only as a vehicle to communicate to
visitors and increase museum access, but also to better understand and
interact with their constituencies.

Online learning can connect visitors to museums and to each other. It
offers individuals and institutions an opportunity to reexamine their
perceived physical and geographic boundaries. As a means of distance
education, online learning can expand the reach of museums to new
audiences and tap resources and staff that are underutilized in traditional
onsite programs, thus providing new educational and economic models.

But online learning in museums offers the possibility of much more.
Beyond its use as a vehicle for distance learning or as an additional
channel of communication or even as a bridge to new visitors, it offers
museums the potential to reconsider their roles as educational institutions. No longer exclusively bound by place or time, online learning can

help museums be better equipped to interact with increasingly dynamic and expanding communities of learners and potential visitors. These on-line communities of learners are forging new types of relationships with museums—ones that are local and personal, yet global and collective.

The models for increased participation, collaboration and community offered by online learning parallel the learner-centric, constructivist approaches currently embraced by museum educators. Knowledge is no longer seen as being "out there" to be acquired, but rather constructed by individuals, groups and communities. As we advance from the Information Age to the Collaboration Age, we are less preoccupied with the task of acquiring facts and more focused on questions of *how* and *why*. We believe that museums should not only "broadcast" to the public at large, but should also "narrowcast" in order to interact with specific communities of learners in new, participatory ways.

Online learning offers an exciting potential for collegial exchange among museum professionals as well as visitors. We see great possibilities for collaboration among our institutions, which opens new doorways for ourselves and our visitors. As we develop and expand learning opportunities within our own institutions, online learning can help us forge new partnerships and collaborations as we strengthen and expand the museum paradigm.

As access to online collections and the open content movement expand through less restrictive copyrights and licensing agreements, new contexts for collections and visitor experiences can be created and explored. This increased access, combined with the power of online learning, can allow many different types of connections, collaborations and communities. Currently, an open courseware model that is being pioneered by a number of international collaborating universities could offer museums a type of commons, or forum, in which to share content with museum visitors and with one another on a global scale. Clearly, no amount of digital resources can replace the experience of being an active participant in an educational program, either online or in-person, but museums should consider how the process-artifacts, recordings and other archived materials from museum-based events can be used in new and innovative ways by our visitors.

Whether museums choose to take an active role in these new online communities of learners or not, they must acknowledge that visitors are already making meaning of both collections and institutions in new ways using online tools. Through direct encounters onsite with museum staff or through informal and collaborative exchanges with their peers online, these visitors select from the resources and tools of the Internet, combine them with their own ideas and experiences and create a different type of ownership of the museum. Although some museums may see online learning and interaction with visitors as a further step towards a loss of control over their collections, we predict that through the development of high-quality online learning opportunities, museums will in fact exert a new leadership in how visitors access and interpret our collections. As responsible stewards, we must use our institutional resources and pedagogical talents to shape and inform these experiences.

Forging and facilitating these new interactions and relationships with visitors take time and commitment. Similar to developing successful in-person learning experiences and programs, online learning requires a great deal of effort, patience, adaptability and flexibility. As we experiment, research and practice, we predict that no single approach will be judged most effective. Nor is any one tool, website or online learning environment without its flaws or drawbacks.

In the end, tools are tools. Hardware and software change. Websites come and go. Whatever we learn, whatever we experience, we consistently find that it too changes and evolves, and our relationship to it changes. What is constant is the dedication and commitment that we as museum professionals have to teaching, to learning and to our visitors.

Authors

WILLIAM B. CROW

Associate Museum Educator

The Metropolitan Museum of Art

William Crow oversees programs for K-12 teachers and offsite school programs at The Metropolitan Museum of Art in New York City. He is also an adjunct instructor of Media Studies in the graduate faculty of The New School, where he has taught online since 2000, including the course *Museums as Media*. As a visual artist, he has shown his work extensively in New York City and abroad. He has been an Artist-in-Residence in the Lower Manhattan Cultural Council's *World Views* Program in the World Trade Center (2000-01), the Millay Colony (2003) and the Bronx Council of the Arts Longwood Program (2005-06) through which artists are provided grants to create online projects. In collaboration with Herminia Din, he developed and taught the Metropolitan's first online workshop for teachers in 2007, *Face to Face: Comparing Portraits*. He holds a BA from Wake Forest, an MFA from Hunter College of The City University of New York, and an MSEd in Leadership in Museum Education from Bank Street College.

HERMINIA WEI-HSIN DIN, PH.D.

Associate Professor of Art Education

Department of Art

University of Alaska - Anchorage

Herminia Wei-Hsin Din is an associate professor of art education at the University of Alaska Anchorage. Previously she was the Web producer at the Children's Museum of Indianapolis and education technologist at the Indianapolis Museum of Art. In the past few years, she has worked with the University of Alaska Museum of the North in Fairbanks on the *LearnAlaska* project, an educational tool to sort, display and share digital museum objects and historical images from the Alaska Digital Archives. In 2005, she facilitated a docent-training program using Internet2 videoconferencing for a traveling exhibit in Alaska, *Light Motifs: American Impressionist Paintings from the Metropolitan Museum of Art.* She serves as program chair and board member of the Media and Technology Committee of AAM. She was also the MUSE Awards Chair for two years. She frequently speaks at national and international conferences on educational media and museum technology. She recently co-edited and contributed to *The Digital Museum: A Think Guide* (2007, AAM Press). She holds a doctorate in art education from Ohio State University.

Index

collaboration, 26–27
  among institutions, 122
  impact on teaching, 94–95
  models, 79
  participatory learning, 82
  teacher/museum staff, 89–91, 95–96
  time and, 91–92
Collaboration Age, 13, 122
collaborators, 39
collections, 122–123
commentary, multimedia, 43
communication, 27–28, 33, 122
  methods, 121
  tools, 2, 33–35
  visitors, 17
community
  experience, 108
  geographically-based, 100
community, online, 100–107
  concepts of, 114
  educational encounter, 106–107
  identifying, 101
  learning power, 107
  motivation and expansion, 108
  technology and, 114
community-building, 26–27, 99–119
Community of Inquiry model, 106, 107–108
community of learners, 32, 122
  case studies, 109–119
concept mapping, 43
Confucius, 78, *97n.1*
conservators, 15
constructivist approach, 122
consumer mentality, 78
costs, 79
Course Management Systems (CMS), 7, 33, 34

courses, fully online or hybrid, 7
courseware, open model, 122–123
Crime Scene Information Technology (CSIT) Forensic Science, 114
Crow, William B., 21, 124

D

delivery methods, 3
depth, asynchronous interaction, 63–64
design, 40
  asynchronous, 41–42
  blended, 42
  synchronous, 42
Dewey, John, 11, *29n.4*, 57–58, 78
Dierking, Lynn, 61
digital drop boxes, 81–82
digital interactions and modalities, "real" experiences vs, 113
digital learning, 6–7, 114
  department, 113–118
digital scrapbooking, 82, *97n.6*
Din, Herminia Wei-Hsin, 21, 125
distance experience, 59
distance learning, 6, 121
documentation, 17, 43

E

ease of use, 16–17
economy, 16
educational encounter, 2, 105–107
  returning to, 84
educator, 15, 62
  methods, 9
Elluminate Live, 21, 26, *29n.11*